FISH·ON·THE·GRILL

FISH · ON · THE · GRILL

MORE THAN 70 ELEGANT, EASY, AND DELECTABLE RECIPES

BARBARA GRUNES AND PHYLLIS MAGIDA

CONTEMPORARY
BOOKS, INC.
CHICAGO ▪ NEW YORK

Library of Congress Cataloging-in-Publication Data

Grunes, Barbara.
  Fish on the grill.

  1. Cookery (Fish)   2. Barbecue cookery.
I. Magida, Phyllis.   II. Title.
TX747.G835   1986   641.6′92   82-2614
ISBN 0-8092-5033-0 (pbk.)

Interior Photos by Paul Natkin
Line Art by Princess Louise El

Published by Contemporary Books, Inc.
180 North Michigan Avenue, Chicago, Illinois 60601
Manufactured in the United States of America
Library of Congress Catalog Card Number: 8-00000
International Standard Book Number: 0-8092-5033-0

Published simultaneously in Canada by Beaverbooks, Ltd.
195 Allstate Parkway, Valleywood Business Park
Markham, Ontario L3R 4T8 Canada

We dedicate this book both to our readers and to all cooks and eaters who love fresh, healthy food made in the best way possible—on the backyard, back porch, or outdoor balcony charcoal grill.

PREFACE

When we set out to write this book, we did not have any of the nagging doubts that cookbook authors often have. We didn't worry that the recipes might be too complicated or time-consuming; they were mostly quick. We didn't worry that the recipes might not be as healthy as possible; fish is low in calories, high in complete protein, low in cholesterol; and charcoal cooking uses as little fat as possible. We didn't worry that we were generating too much kitchen cleanup; the dishes often all but cooked themselves. We didn't even worry that a cookbook of this nature—fish made on the grill—had been written before. It hadn't.

In a sense, you could call this a conflict-free book. Fresh fish, made on the outdoor grill, was and is the cuisine of the future. And as we worked out and tested each recipe, two things that we had sensed, but had not articulated, became clear: First, fresh, charcoal-grilled fish is so delicious that it often doesn't need a sauce, but adding a sauce makes it even more delicious. Second, each type of fish, delicious and individual as it might be, is not so many light-years away in taste from many other types of fresh fish, so the sauces are often interchangeable, mixable, and matchable. In other words, just about any sauce in the book goes with just about any kind of fish.

Therefore, we designed the recipes to be flexible. Try them as written, then go ahead and experiment! But be sure to consult the fish chart on pages 12–13, which indicates the broad range of fish varieties and possible substitutions. Create and enjoy, as we did in developing this book for you.

INTRODUCTION

Fresh grilled fish is the food of the future—it's speedy and often easy to make; it's healthy, sophisticated, and delicious!

Part I of this book provides fish grilling fundamentals, such as grill and fuel selection, how to buy fresh fish, and general tips on amounts, cooking times, and substitutions. In this section, you'll also find a chapter called "5-Minute Fish," which will provide you with mix and match guidelines for creating your own *quick* and impressive recipes.

Part II includes recipes for a number of different kinds of seafood ranging from salmon, sole, and shrimp to the less familiar ono and mahimahi.

These recipes have been chosen from several different perspectives. First, we wanted to use different varieties of fish so we could explore the textural possibilities available. The fish used in our recipes range from the very delicate, such as sole, to the sturdier varieties like swordfish. We also wanted to explore the different cuts of fish. Like pasta, which many people insist changes flavor and texture with its shape (i.e. manicotti is said to have a different flavor than linguini), we think that a fillet of fish has a different quality than a fish steak, that fish on a skewer is drastically different from fish grilled whole.

The recipes reflect the healthy and exciting innovativeness so prevalent in cooking today. You'll find these recipes both flavorful and light, with influences ranging from Cajun to California fresh, from Thai through Southwestern American. We include recipes from a number of cuisines, not only to supply a choice of ethnic flavors available in the repertoire, but also because certain cuisines handle grilling fish especially well. The Korean marinated fish, for example, is characteristic of what is done with fish in that country; and besides being very interesting, it's very good.

And, of course, we wanted to include recipes that would give you a choice of time spent in preparation. So we have included a 5-minute chapter that literally allows almost instant preparation. While most of the recipes in this book are not at all time-consuming—one of the beauties of grilled fish—for the days when you have afternoons available we have included longer, more complicated recipes, like shrimp tandoori, where the shrimp marinate for some time before being cooked.

We also included recipes for a few side dishes to go with the grilled fish—such as baked beans with ham (the only time meat is even mentioned in the book), hush puppies, and cole slaw, among others.

But before you can cook the fish, you have to buy it, set up the grill, and light the coals—so we begin with the basics. Read on to learn precisely how to get those fish out of the frying pan and onto that fire.

CONTENTS

PART II: THE RECIPES

FISH·ON·THE GRILL

PART I
THE FUNDAMENTALS

1
THE TOOLS: GRILLS, FUELS, AND MORE

In regular indoor cooking, you have to know your oven and your pots and pans. The same holds true in grilling; you have to know your grill, your tools, and your fuel. This section will help you familiarize yourself with these elements of grilling.

Minimally you will need only the simplest equipment: a grill, some fuel, a way to start the fire, and, of course, a piece of fish. Maximally, you can have every type of skewer and basket. You are limited only by your imagination.

GRILLS

There are basically three types of grills, although many variations and attachments appear regularly on the market. All of these are applicable and workable for grilling fish, but none are any better than any other, providing you know how to use your grill.

The Basic Brazier

The simplest brazier type consists basically of a pan with raised sides to hold the fire and a grill over the fire to hold the food. It has no cover to hold in the smoke and no vents to help control the heat. Sometimes it sits on legs; sometimes it's laid flat on the ground. It is manually heated with charcoal, never gas or electricity. This type of grill sometimes costs very little in drugstores and supermarkets. It is very satisfactory for all fish (and most other foods). It is not recommended for whole birds and roasts—foods that need longer, slower cooking.

Another type of grill consists of a brazier with a hood. The hood may be merely a shield from the wind and rain, or it can be more elaborate, containing vents to help regulate the heat (shutting off the air helps keep the fire under control), which circulates around the food in a manner similar to the heat circulation in an oven. A cover also increases the amount of smoke circulating around the food, resulting in food with a smokier flavor. It hastens cooking, too, since heat is reflected off the inside surface of the cover.

Round grills with round covers are called *barbecue kettles*. Rectangular grills with rectangular covers (sometimes they have wheels) are often called *grill wagons*. Covered grills most often use charcoal for fuel, though many outdoor cooks today substitute aromatic hardwood chunks or add hardwood to a charcoal base.

A more elaborate type of brazier with a hood is heated by gas or electricity. The heating element is often surrounded by a permanent bed of lava rock or contains a plate to catch the drippings. These grills can be either freestanding or installed permanently in the backyard or on a patio (and, in some cases, in a well-ventilated kitchen or fireplace). When the fat from the food drips onto the bed of volcanic rock, it sizzles and sends up smoke, which helps flavor the food. Some manufacturers of gas and electric grills feel that the smoke from the sizzling fat is wholly responsible for the characteristic barbecue flavor. Our feeling, however, is that the sizzling fat smoke makes up only part of the grilled flavor, that the best grilled food results from a combination of sizzling fat smoke and charcoal and/or wood smoke.

The Hibachi

One ethnic grill, called a Japanese hibachi, has become very popular in this country. These cunning little cookers have no legs, which means they can be set up right on the outdoor table where you will be eating. Hibachis are also at their best when set up on fire escapes, back stairs, and rooftops, since they can be easily withdrawn when faced with complaining landlords or neighbors. It's in the nature of the hibachi that it is very small—too small, unfortunately, to make a grilled dinner for four; but it will accommodate two or three adequately. Hibachis can often be quite expensive.

The Water Smoker

The water smoker, a third type of grill, functions differently from the regular charcoal grill. Food put in it to smoke is usually

4

left for several hours—unlike the grilled recipes we suggest in this book, which take only minutes to cook. Water smokers, which consist of a firebox, a pan of water, a grill, and a cover, are at their best when smoking large pieces of food, such as pheasant, duck, turkey, large cuts of meat, and, of course, whole fish. It also accommodates fish steaks or fillets nicely. This grill is perfect for the large fish you catch yourself, bring home, and put on the smoker the same day.

When purchasing a grill, consider the area where you will be cooking. If you have a small balcony, you will need a small grill. With a larger space you have more options. But if you are keen on cooking a whole fish, you may have to juggle the size of the grill with the size of the fish you want to cook.

Grilling, whether fish or meat, is probably one of the oldest cooking methods. Grill manufacturers have had a lot of time to perfect the equipment and we recommend all types of grills.

FUEL

Charcoal

There are two basic kinds of charcoal: pure hardwood charcoal, which is sold in lump form, and charcoal that has been compressed into briquet form. Pure hardwood charcoal is made by burning hardwood until it's dry and porous. Pure hardwood charcoal is always marked as such on the box (sometimes with the name of the wood or woods also indicated) and is more expensive than briquets. The smoke that comes from pure hardwood charcoal has a slightly more savory, woody scent and is superior to that from briquets.

Briquets may be labeled simply *briquets, charcoal briquets, compressed wood charcoal,* or something similar. They may be made entirely of charred pieces of wood, or the wood may be compressed mechanically with charred paper and/or sawdust, all of which is held together with some kind of artificial mastic such as a petroleum product. Unfortunately, there is no standard of identity for briquets, so the quality of the smoke they produce when burning varies widely. The best briquets contain very little mastic—just enough to hold them together—and, in the bag, smell faintly of burnt wood. Avoid those that, in the bag, have an artificial odor such as motor oil; these may give off the same odor when they burn. The smoke that comes from burning the best of the impure hardwood briquets is pleasant and acceptable.

In terms of flavor, when grilling a fish fillet or fish steak, some people insist it doesn't really matter whether you use pure hardwood charcoal or other kinds of briquets (provided they're of good quality) since fish pieces cook so quickly that they absorb only a small amount of smoky flavor. Of course, if you're cooking a large, whole fish in a smoker or a covered grill for a long period of time, you may want to use the pure stuff, since a whole fish takes a longer cooking time and so absorbs more smoky flavor.

But for the sake of purity, many people choose pure hardwood charcoal. After all, they reason, a fresh piece of fish is pure and natural, and grilling is a pure and natural cooking method, so why adulterate the finished product by using impure charcoal? For most of us, good-quality briquets are very acceptable; but if you have a particularly sensitive palate, you'll want to use the pure hardwood stuff.

Aromatics

Whether you use a pure hardwood charcoal or plain briquets, you can intensify the smoky flavor of your fish by throwing various kinds of aromatics onto your hot coals before cooking. Most aromatics are available in the form of fruitwood or hardwood cuttings and include mesquite, hickory, oak, apple, maple, and cherry wood chips. Each wood gives its own flavor to the smoke, and you may want to experiment with some of them or mix and match.

Hickory, for example, has a strong, identifiable flavor and a pungent aroma; oak is similar to hickory, but slightly less pungent and a little sweeter. Cherry and other fruitwoods such as apple produce a particularly sweet-smelling smoke and so are effective with more delicately flavored fish.

Another wood that recently has gained popularity in America is mesquite, which is available both in hardwood charcoal form and in chip form. At this moment, many restaurants all over America are advertising their "swordfish over mesquite," using either the charcoal or a handful of the chips. Thicker, sturdier kinds of fish, such as shark and swordfish, are enhanced by mesquite smoke.

Other common aromatics used in America include stalks of fresh herbs such as thyme, tarragon, basil, fennel, bay leaves, rosemary, sage, and juniper twigs, which can be sprinkled over the hot coals right before setting the fish on the grill. (Some buffs tie stalks of fresh herbs into a small bunch, then use this as a basting brush during cooking.) In China, barbecuers throw tea leaves or pieces of orange peel onto the hot coals. And in France, they might substitute grapevine cuttings or a handful of garlic cloves.

Some barbecue buffs enjoy dispensing with charcoal entirely and using just aromatic hardwoods or corncobs as fuel. This is fine for pork or beef. But we do not recommend this with fish because the delicate flavor of the fish would be overpowered by the strong, assertive fragrances of the smoke given off by some hardwoods alone.

Wood chips should be soaked for several minutes (follow package directions) before throwing them onto the hot coals, as this will prolong their smoking life. If the chips float when you put them into the pan of water, simply lay a plate over the top to submerge them.

Aromatic woods, charcoal, and other fuels are so widespread that most are available at supermarkets, specialty shops, some hardware shops, and even department stores and pharmacies all over the country. Once you bring your fuel home, store it in a moisture-free area, away from your furnace or heaters.

Electricity and Gas

If you have an electric or gas grill, you can (and should) throw aromatics onto the bed of lava rock or onto the bottom of the grill. (Remember, we said earlier that the smoke produced by the burning fat of the cooking food is only part of the deliciousness of grilling fish; the other part is produced by the smoke from the fuel.) If you do this, though, be sure to turn your grill upside down to shake out the ash at the end of the barbecue season.

MISCELLANEOUS EQUIPMENT

You don't need special equipment for grilling. You can get away with a grill, some charcoal, some starter, a wire brush for cleaning the grill, and a few tools found around any kitchen: a fork, a spatula (the kind used for flipping pancakes), a pastry brush, and a regular pair of kitchen tongs (the kind that were formerly used to handle sterilized baby bottles).

But if you decide to buy special equipment, then we recommend certain types—ones we have found to work very efficiently. A *long-handled fork*, for example, is not only efficient, it keeps you from burning yourself. And instead of buying a pastry brush, we recommend a *large paint brush* (good quality so the hairs don't come out). A real painter's paint brush is larger, thicker (it will hold more basting butter or sauce), and more efficient than a pastry brush.

Although many *long-handled spatulas*, designed especially for grilling, are available, we recommend those with wide blades. Otherwise, you're better off with a regular kitchen spatula. If you decide to buy *tongs*, buy spring-loaded, stainless-steel tongs. Because they're spring-loaded, they're easier to handle than the ordinary found-around-the-house variety.

Less common pieces of equipment include *skewers* for shish kabob and *fish baskets*. Skewers can be any length, but avoid those with wooden handles. They look pretty when you buy them, but after a couple of uses the wood finish chars and scorches. Four 10-inch-long all-metal skewers will serve you very well. Eight would be better. If you add an additional eight 20-inch skewers, you'll have all you'll ever need. Whatever size you buy, be sure the skewers are not round. If they are round, the fish chunks will slip when you turn the skewer. Each skewer should have four flat sides.

Fish baskets—wire baskets with covers, which adjust to the fish's thickness, attached to long handles—come in a variety of sizes and shapes. Some are rectangular, some are shaped like a fish. The ones we recommend are rectangular and will hold fish fillets, fish steaks, or whole fish. Fish baskets are useful in turning fish. Secured in a basket, the fish will not flop around when the basket is turned. Baskets can be quite expensive—as high as $20 or more. But if you shop carefully, you should be able to find one for under $12.

You will, of course, be purchasing something with which to start your fire. You can use an *electric starter* (which requires an electric outlet), *a small chimney, a paraffin starter* (a piece of compressed wood or paper with a paraffin base), or the commercial *liquid chemical lighter* available everywhere. But before choosing your starter, be sure to check its aroma. Some chemical starters have an incredibly strong odor that lasts.

2
A COMPENDIUM OF FISH FACTS

HOW TO BUY FISH

This is the most important technique you can master.

Go to a fish market with the largest possible turnover, then make friends with your fishmonger. Ask him for the freshest possible fish. If you want to cook fresh trout, but the grouper is fresher, buy the grouper and change your recipe plans. Freshness is more important than anything else in buying fish.

To choose a fresh whole fish: Look for crystal-clear, bright eyes and gills that show a little bit of red underneath. If the eyes are cloudy, or if the gills are brown or darker underneath, the fish is too old. Also, the skin should look fresh and glistening; if it has begun to turn gray or fade, the fish is old. With your finger, push a small dent into the side of the fish. If the fish is fresh, the flesh will be elastic and firm enough to spring back, filling up the dent. If the dent remains, the fish is too old. Lastly, open the fish up and smell the inside, where the intestines have been removed. If the fish is fresh, it will have no odor beyond the faint smell of seaweed.

Fish steaks and fillets should feel firm and moist to the touch, not spongy or dry. The flesh should have a translucent, clear look and not be at all milky and white. If possible, ask the fishmonger to cut the fish steaks to order from a fish you have chosen. Fillets should be firm, translucent, and not white—whiteness is a sign of age. Run your finger over the surface of the fillet. If you get a slimy, sticky mucus on your finger, the fish is old.

Make friends with your fishmonger! Fresh fish are available at a number of places: supermarkets, specialty fish shops, and fish farms (where you catch your own). Wherever you buy, be sure to check the fish for freshness. Also, look first at the fish caught in your area—they are probably cheaper and fresher than imported varieties. In the past, fish and shellfish were always shipped frozen. This is only sometimes true today, and frozen does not necessarily mean tasteless. Check with your fishmonger. Ask him for the freshest and best.

When possible, buy fish with the head, the tail, and the backbone intact. Cooking a fish with the head and tail will seal in the juices, and the backbone acts as a heat conductor, which is important when cooking a large fish.

How Much Fish to Buy per Person

The chart below will tell you how much fish to allow per person. Although most dietitians recommend less protein per meal, we have upped the servings for three reasons: (1) We are referring to uncooked fish, which weighs more than cooked fish. (2) Fish eating is relatively new in this country, and since your guests are used to beef, you might want to serve them slightly larger portions of fish. (3) Americans are used to large amounts of animal protein, and you don't want your guests to feel that you are skimping on the entree.

How Much Fish to Buy Per Person, Per Serving	
Fish (whole)	Buy small individual 1-lb. fish per person. Figure 1 lb. or slightly less per person when portions are part of a larger fish (3-3½ lb. stuffed fish will serve 3-4 people amply).
Fish Fillets	7 oz. per person
Fish Steaks	7 oz. per person
Fish Kabobs	7 oz. per person

FISH SPECIES

Fish come naturally in many guises: fatty, moderate, or lean; freshwater (more small, tiny bones) or saltwater (fewer small, annoying bones); cool-water fish (with richer flavor caused by higher fat content) and warm-water fish; and don't forget the textural differences, ranging from tender, delicately melting types to fish so firm and chewy that you'll feel like you're eating beef.

The chart on pages 12–13 includes fat content, texture, and calories per 100 grams (about 3½ oz., raw) of the wide variety of fish you'll find in this book. Calorie and fat content charts are based on USDA figures. Textural comments are made by authors and refer to cooked texture. When a fish is designated fatty, this means it contains over 10 percent fat; when a fish is designated moderate, it has 6–10 percent fat; when a fish is designated lean, this means it has less than 5 percent fat. While all fish species are relatively low in fat, for those on very low-fat, low-calorie diets, serve the portions designated in the preceding chart but choose one of the lean species listed on pages 12–13

When you're beginning to experiment with fish, you may want to substitute a fish of similar flavor and texture in a recipe. Almost every fish is interchangeable in our recipes. Kabobs are the exception; soft-fleshed fish will not stay on the skewer. The chart below shows which types are similar to others, as well as nutritional information.

HOW TO STORE FISH

Try to use the fish the day you bring it home. But if you must store the fish overnight, begin by filling a pan with water and setting it in the freezer. While you wait for the water in the pan to freeze, rinse the fish in cold, salted water and pat it dry with paper towels. Rewrap it in clean waxed paper, then place it in a clean plastic bag and secure it with a twister seal. Set it on a plate and cover both the plate and the fish with the plastic wrap; refrigerate temporarily.

When the water is frozen, remove the pan from the freezer. Place the plate with the fish on the ice and set it in the refrigerator overnight. It will stay extra cold until you are ready to use it.

Fat Content, Texture, Flavor and Calories in Fish Species

FISH	FAT CONTENT	TEXTURE & FLAVOR	CALORIES per 100 g	SUBSTITUTIONS
Bass, black sea	low	med. firm mild	100	red sea bass, striped sea bass, grouper, halibut, mahi mahi, rockfish, snapper, tilefish, monkfish, porgy
Bass, red sea	low	med. firm mild	90	same as black sea bass
Bass, striped	low	med. firm mild	90	red sea bass, black sea bass, grouper, halibut, orange roughy, ocean perch, rockfish, tilefish
Bluefish	mod. high	delicate distinctive	110	mackerel, kingfish, whitefish, lake trout, rainbow trout
Buffalofish	high	med. distinctive	215	red sea bass, black sea bass, snapper, yellowtail, butterfish
Catfish freshwater	mod. high	med. firm sweet	115	orange roughy, ocean perch, small rockfish, walleye pike
Cod	low	delicate mild	75	scrod (the same as cod), haddock, pollack, lingcod, black cod, flounder
Grouper	low	firm mild	95	black sea bass, red sea bass, snapper, halibut, walleye pike, tautog, tilefish
Halibut	mod. high	med. firm sweet	110	black sea bass, red sea bass, snapper, mahi mahi, yellowtail, tilefish
Mackerel	high	med. distinctive	175	bluefish, rainbow trout, brook trout, whitefish, lake trout, yellowtail, sea trout
Mahi mahi	mod. low	med. firm mild	90	black sea bass, red sea bass, snapper, ono, salmon, yellowtail, sea trout
Ono	med.	firm mild	120	swordfish, shark, kingfish, rockfish, snapper, grouper, yellowtail, pompano
Orange Roughy	low	med. very mild	75	sole, catfish, scrod (cod), haddock, pollack, small rockfish, ocean perch, turbot, flounder, tilapia
Ocean Perch	mod. high	med. mild	105	walleye pike, orange roughy, flounder, turbot, small rockfish, tilapia, sea trout
Pompano	high	med. mildly distinct	165	ono, yellowtail, kingfish, swordfish, bluefish, mackerel
Redfish	low	med. firm mild	90	same as black sea bass
Rockfish	low	med. firm mild	90	snapper, grouper, catfish, ocean perch, sea bass, tilefish, monkfish, sea trout
Salmon Atlantic	high	med. firm mildly distinct	220	All salmon can be substituted for one another. lake trout, whitefish, rainbow trout, brook trout
Salmon Chinook	high	med. firm mildly distinct	185	Same as Atlantic Salmon
Salmon Sockeye	high	med. firm mildly distinct	155	Same as Atlantic Salmon
Scrod	low	delicate mild	75	same as cod
Shark	mod. low	firm mildly distinct	85	swordfish, ono (wahoo), tuna, marlin
Sole	low	delicate sweet	85	orange roughy, ocean perch, flounder, turbot, tilapia
Snapper, red	mod. low	med. firm mild	110	same as black sea bass

FISH	FAT CONTENT	TEXTURE & FLAVOR	CALORIES per 100 g	SUBSTITUTIONS
Swordfish	mod. high	firm mildly distinct	125	ono (wahoo), shark, tuna, marlin
Trout, brook	mod. high	med. mildly distinct	110	rainbow trout, lake trout, salmon, walleye pike, whitefish, crappie, sunfish, haddock, pollack
Trout, rainbow	high	med. mildly distinct	130	same as brook trout
Trout, lake	high	med. mildly distinct	165	same as brook trout
Tuna, bluefin	high	firm mildly distinct	160	swordfish, shark, ono (wahoo), any other tuna, marlin
Tuna, yellowfin	mod. high	firm mildly distinct	125	same as bluefin tuna
Yellowtail Pacific coast	mod. low	med. firm mild	100	snapper, grouper, kingfish, ono (wahoo), pompano, rockfish, tautog
Walleye pike	low	med. firm mildly distinct	90	flounder, rainbow trout, brook trout, ocean perch, catfish, lake perch, crappie, sunfish, tilapia
Whitefish, lake	high	delicate mildly distinct	165	same as brook trout

In general fish are not high in cholesterol.

Fat Content, Texture, Flavor and Calories in Shellfish Species

SHELLFISH	FAT CONTENT	TEXTURE & FLAVOR	CALORIES per 100 g
Clams	low	firm distinctive	63
Crab	mod. low	med. firm mildly distinct	85
Lobster	low	firm mildly distinct	100
Mussels	low	med. mildly distinct	77
Oysters	mod. low	med. distinctive	80
Scallops	low	med. mild	80
Shrimp	low	med. firm mildly distinct	95

Latest research indicates that the cholesterol levels of shellfish are negligible to moderate at most.

3

HOW TO COOK FISH ON THE GRILL

Grilling fish, although quick and easy, does demand a certain amount of attention. Fish overcooks easily—too easily. If you direct your attention from the grill for just a moment or two, you may find yourself with a dry-on-the-inside, charred-on-the-outside piece of fish. Although we have given the grilling times as accurately as possible in the recipes, remember that grills vary, the distance between the charcoal briquets and the grating varies, charcoals vary, and the heat varies too, since you can't set the temperature on a charcoal grill as you can with an oven. Add to this the fact that thickness varies from fish to fish and that the temperature of the fish, whether fresh from the refrigerator or at room temperature, varies too, as does the weather. All of these things are going to affect your charcoal grilling of fish. So our advice to all fish-on-the-grill cooks is to *pay attention* for the few minutes the fish is on the grill. If you do, your results are all but guaranteed.

DIRECT vs. INDIRECT HEAT

Once you've chosen your grill, your fuel, and your recipe, decide whether you want to cook your fish by the direct heat or the indirect heat method. In the direct method, the fish is cooked directly over the heat. The ashy white charcoal is spread out over the bottom of the grill in an even layer, and the fish is then laid on the grill over the direct heat. An advantage of the direct cooking method is that the fish cooks very quickly. Disadvantages include having to take extra precautions and care so the fish won't burn and expecting only a minimum of smoky flavor to permeate the fish flesh because of the shortened cooking time.

In the indirect method, the ashy white charcoal is divided into two small banks on either side of the grill. The fish is laid in the center of the grill, away from the direct heat of the charcoal. (Some people lay a pan in the center of the kettle bottom to catch the drippings.) The fish is then cooked—partly by the heat, partly by the hot smoke. If you cover the grill, the smoky flavor will be intensified. The advantages of the indirect method include slow cooking so that you don't have to watch the fish quite so carefully plus maximum exposure to the flavorful smoke.

Disadvantages include a slightly longer cooking time and the necessity for a cover so that the fish will absorb maximum smoke fragrance.

STARTING A FIRE

Once you've decided on your grilling method, you may line the grill with heavy-duty foil, if desired; this makes for easier cleanup but is not necessary. If you poke a few holes in the foil and cover the grill for the few moments it takes to cook the fish, the fish will still absorb the delicious smoky flavor. And this insures easy, intact removal.

Another alternative: you may wish to use a special piece of equipment called a *fish basket* (see Chapter 2). This consists of a wire basket attached to a long handle and allows the fish to be turned without its falling apart. If you do use a fish basket, be sure to grease it thoroughly.

Start the fire 45 minutes to an hour before you plan to grill so that when you are ready to begin cooking, the charcoal will be covered with a thick layer of grayish-white ash. Pile the briquets into a pyramid in the center of the grill. An average-size kettle (18–22 inches) needs only 30–35 briquets if you are using the direct cooking method. If you're using the indirect method, you may want to add an extra 5–10 briquets. Light the charcoal using one of the methods described in Chapter 2.

All recipes in this book were tested by the direct method of grilling. If you want to use the indirect method, add a few minutes to your calculated cooking time. The times given for each recipe, again, are approximate. Grilling time will vary with each experience, but once you've learned to judge the fish's doneness using the chart and instructions on page 17, you should have no trouble calculating times.

How long you'll have to wait before the fire is ready for cooking depends on a number of factors, but you'll know it's ready when the charcoal is covered with a fine layer of white ash. At this point, the ashy charcoal will produce a steady, even heat—perfect for grilling. It is the direct infrared radiation from the coals that is supposed to do the major part of the cooking; never a direct flame. If you cook anything, but particularly fish, over flaming coals, you will have trouble preventing it from burning.

Spread out the briquets to accommodate your cooking method. Then carefully brush a little shortening or oil on the grating (don't use butter—it burns too quickly). This step is imperative; fish is delicate and may stick to the grill when you try to turn or remove it. And be sure your grill is clean. Fish has a tendency to stick to a dirty grill.

COOKING THE FISH

Remove the fish from the refrigerator. It is important that the fish be very cold when put on the greased grating. The cold will slow the cooking time and allow the fish to absorb as much of the smoky flavor as possible. Do not salt the fish before cooking. Salting draws some of the moisture out of the flesh and toughens it.

Set a pan of water near the grill and watch the charcoal carefully during cooking. If it flares up into a direct flame, immediately sprinkle water over it to quench the flames. Incidentally, there's some indication that doing this produces a steam that helps keep the fish moist.

Fish flesh sticks to metal, so don't forget to oil your fish well on both sides, to oil the grill, to oil the inside of the grill basket, and to insert lemon or lime slices at a few places between the fish and the grill when feasible.

To figure out the approximate grilling time for a fish steak, a thick fish fillet, a whole stuffed fish, or a kabob, measure the fish at the thickest point (right behind the head) and allow 10 minutes of direct grilling time for each inch of thickness. When using the indirect method, allow 15–18 minutes per inch. Remember, however, that this rule is qualified by the temperature of the air and the fish, by the heat of the grill, and by the distance between the coals and the food. So *watch your fish carefully*—from one minute after you put it on the grill until it's done. When the fish is almost done, you will get the best results if you stand there and give it your full attention for the last few minutes. Use the following chart as a guide to cooking times.

Ready or Not?

We cannot stress enough the importance of paying attention to the fish while it cooks. You don't have to hover over the grill constantly, but check the fish regularly. A well-cooked piece of fish looks opaque. The texture is right when the fish begins to flake when tested with a fork. If it is already flaky, it is overdone. Fish, like steak, continues to cook for a moment or two after it's taken from the grill.

How Long on the Grill*

Small Whole Fish	6-9 minutes on each side
Large Whole Fish	11-20 minutes on each side (or even longer occasionally, if fish is thicker or stuffed)
Fillets	4-8 minutes on each side (or longer occasionally, when fillet is very thick). Turn only if flesh is firm and thick enough to do so.
Steaks (1 inch thick)	5 minutes on each side for a total of 10 minutes. If fish is thicker, increase cooking time according to thickness (10 minutes per inch).
Kabobs	Most kabobs are cut 1 to 1½ inches thick and will take about 9 to 15 minutes. Cook them 3 minutes on each side, then turn. Continue cooking and turning until they're done.

*NOTE: This chart is based on the direct cooking method. If you use the indirect method, increase the cooking time 2-4 minutes.

Lay the fish on the greased grating. If you're cooking a fillet, be sure to lay it skin-side down on the grill. The skin, incidentally, helps protect the flesh from burning and drying out.

Check a whole fish for doneness by examining the thickest part—right in back of the head. Another test for a whole fish is to leave the side fins on and, when you think the fish is done, test it by gently pulling on a fin. If it comes off with only a gentle pull, it's done. You could also insert an instant read thermometer into the thickest part of the whole fish. It should read about 135°F. If it reads higher, take the fish off the grill immediately. Whatever you do, be aware of the fact that you have a delicate, easily overcooked piece of deliciousness on your grill. Watch it accordingly.

Don't turn your fillets. They can cook fully just by having one side exposed to the fuel and probably will fall apart if you try to turn them. Fish steaks and whole fish can be turned, but again, care should be exercised.

From Grill to Platter

To remove the fish (whether fillet, steak, or whole fish) from the grill, grease a spatula well. If the fish sticks in spite of the oil, carefully and slowly loosen it with a gentle back-and-forth motion, using the spatula. You may want to use two greased spatulas to remove a large fish. You may serve your fish on slightly warmed platters and plates. But do not let them get too hot or the fish may continue cooking after being removed from the grill.

TIPS FOR COOKING FISH ON THE GRILL

- Throughout this book, you'll find statements like "fish is done when it begins to flake when tested with a fork." This means, specifically, when pressure is applied with a fork to the thickest part of the fish, the fish will easily split along its natural separations.
- You'll have a better chance of removing delicate fillets from the grill if you cut them so that they're no larger than 4 inches square.
- When grilling a fillet with the tail section, fold this section under; this will help even out the thickness of the fish and so make possible a more uniformly cooked fillet.
- Today's trend is to undercook fish, rather than cook it until dry. Fish should be moist and opaque. It should have just lost its translucency.
- If you want to take extra precautions to keep a piece of fish moist, marinate it in a plastic bag full of several spoonfuls of oil and turn it regularly before cooking. When it comes to grilling it, however, don't forget to give it your full attention. Marinating fish in oil will not ensure that it will not overcook.
- You'll find more tips throughout the body of this book.

4
FIVE-MINUTE FISH

Your boss keeps you late at the office, despite the fact that your newest boyfriend or girlfriend is coming to dinner for the first time. Never mind. Forget the dinner you planned. Stop at the fish store and buy some fillets of whatever kind is freshest (see tips, page 9), then hurry home with confidence. Your dinner should take only minutes to make.

It really is almost that easy. There are, however, a few things to keep in mind:

- Once you're at the fish store, be sure to choose a quick-cooking cut. A thin fillet, such as sole or whitefish, will take just minutes on the grill and doesn't need to be turned. A fish steak also cooks in a short time. If you're really rushed, don't buy a whole fish; it takes too long. And don't buy fish for shish kabob, it takes several minutes just to thread the fish and vegetables on skewers.
- Plan your meal on the way to the fish store. Plan side dishes and sauces or butters that are made of ingredients you have on hand. It helps if you've anticipated a possible emergency and stockpiled ingredients—such as olives (needed for our olive spread) or dried tarragon (needed for our sole with tarragon)—for just such emergencies.
- Also, if you're a beginning cook and estimating how long a dish will take you, the time you figure should be doubled or tripled. What the experienced cook can put together in 5 minutes, may take the novice as much as 20 minutes.
- When you're pressed for time and need a quick marinade, run to the refrigerator and take out your leftover salad dressing. Pour this into a bowl, add the fish fillet and let it sit for 30 minutes. If the dressing tastes good on salad, it will taste good on grilled fish.

To start you off, we've included sauce recipes to accompany a variety of fish, all of which can be made very quickly. There are also a couple of almost-instant recipes, for those who must have guidelines. So rush home, heat those coals, whip together a quick sauce, throw the fish on the grill and ta-da! An elegant repast.

19

TIPS FOR MAKING SIMPLY SUBLIME BUTTER SAUCES

- You can invent your own delicious butter-based sauces by mixing almost anything that has a strong, hearty flavor—be it fish roe in a jar, anchovies, savory herbs (tarragon, rosemary, sage, thyme, etc.), capers, horseradish, mustard, garlic, or shallots—with enough butter at room temperature (for a spreading consistency). Then, when your fish is hot off the grill, transfer it to a serving dish, put a dollop or two of seasoned butter on the fish (it will melt), and serve immediately. Be sure to pass the remaining butter mixture.

- Nut butters go wonderfully with all the fish varieties in this book. What's a nut butter? It's finely chopped or ground nuts combined with softened butter which can be spread on fish. Try pecan butter, walnut butter, or cashew butter. Add a squeeze of lemon juice, pinch of salt, and a half teaspoon or so of chopped onion and you've got something special. Serve it as a log, for guests to slice, or just put a dollop on each piece of hot fish and wait for it to melt. Delicious!

- Herbs and herb butters go well with all types of fish in this book. You may want to mix a few herbs together, fresh or dried, and combine them with butter to taste. Parsley adds a green note and combines well with almost anything. Parsley is especially effective when used fresh, even when combined with dried herbs, because its overall effect is freshness.

- When added judiciously with dried herbs, chives act as a flavor compliment, adding pungency. A small amount of very finely chopped onion or green onion will do the same.

- When mixing herb butters, be sure the butter is soft, room temperature, so the herbs combine evenly. As soon as you get home, take the butter out of the refrigerator, measure it, cut it into pieces, and place it in a bowl in a warm place (maybe right near the stove). When speed is important, nothing is more exasperating than trying to stir something into cold butter.

- If you really have no time, not even for the butter to soften at room temperature, melt it in a pan over low heat with the herbs. Then spoon it over the just-grilled fish. It works as well as the more solid varieties.

CLARIFIED BUTTER

Clarified butter does not burn readily and is very useful in preparing sauces.

¼ pound unsalted butter

Melt butter in small saucepan over low heat. Skim off the white foam that forms on the top of the butter. Pour the remaining butter into a covered glass container, cool, and refrigerate until needed.

LEMON BUTTER

Lemon butter is delicious with any kind of fish in this book.

4 tablespoons (½ stick) butter, room temperature
2 teaspoons minced fresh parsley
2 tablespoons fresh lemon juice
1 teaspoon grated lemon zest

Cream butter until soft. Add minced parsley, lemon juice, and zest. Continue beating until butter is fluffy. Can be stored.

Yield: 4 servings

TROPICAL FRUIT GARNISH

1 papaya or mango, peeled, seeded, and sliced
1 large firm banana, sliced
2 kiwifruit, peeled and sliced
2 tablespoons fresh orange juice

Toss all ingredients in a large mixing bowl. Spoon the fruit mixture over grilled fish fillet or steaks.

Yield: 4 servings

BASIL MAYONNAISE

This lovely mayonnaise will compliment any seafood, especially leftover shrimp. The sauce is improved by using homemade mayonnaise for a base (see recipe, p. 102). However, commercial mayonnaise is fine when you have last-minute company.

If you find yourself with a piece of cold, leftover grilled fish, a sandwich spread with basil mayonnaise will turn a leftover into a delight.

1   cup mayonnaise
¼   cup lightly packed fresh basil leaves
¼   teaspoon each: salt, white pepper

Process mayonnaise, basil leaves, salt, and pepper in a food processor fitted with a steel blade, until smooth. Taste and adjust seasonings. Place basil mayonnaise in a covered container and chill until ready to serve.

Yield: 1¼ cups

BEER SAUCE

This hearty, but easy, sauce goes well with any fish, particularly the heartier varieties. Try it on a cold day (sure, you can grill in the cold—all you need is a coat and a few minutes time).

1   cup mayonnaise
¼   cup catsup
¼   cup dark beer
2   teaspoons prepared mustard
½   teaspoon fresh lemon juice
¼   teaspoon, or to taste, white horseradish

Combine mayonnaise, catsup, beer, mustard, lemon juice, and horseradish in a small bowl. Cover and refrigerate until ready to serve.

Yield: 1½ cups

None of the recipes in this book are time-consuming; however, these recipes are particularly simple and quick—yet impressive.

SOLE WITH TARRAGON

4 7-ounce sole, flounder, or gray sole fillets
Oil for greasing fish basket
Melted butter
White pepper
Crumbled, dried tarragon
Carrot curls for garnish
Cherry tomatoes for garnish
½ pound green grapes for garnish

Arrange sole fillets on a prepared double-hinged grill basket or on a sheet of aluminum foil with some air holes. Brush with melted butter. Sprinkle fish with white pepper and tarragon. Sprinkle 2 tablespoons of tarragon directly on hot coals. Place fish on prepared grill and cook about 4 minutes, until it begins to flake when tested with a fork. Brush with butter during grilling. Place fish on individual dishes and garnish with carrot curls, cherry tomatoes, and small clusters of green grapes.

Yield: 4 servings

LAKE TROUT MEUNIERE

FISH
4   10-ounce lake trout
Melted butter
2   lemons, sliced thin
Oil for greasing fish basket
4   tablespoons minced fresh parsley for garnish

MEUNIERE SAUCE
8   tablespoons (1 stick) butter
¼   teaspoon freshly ground pepper
Juice of ½ lemon
Minced fresh parsley for garnish

1. *Grill trout:* Brush individual trout with melted butter and put lemon slices in cavities. Arrange fish in a prepared double-hinged fish basket and grill trout for 3–4 minutes. Brush fish with butter, turn, and grill 2–3 minutes depending on thickness of fish, until it begins to flake when tested with a fork. Arrange trout on individual plates.

2. *Make sauce:* While trout is grilling, melt 8 tablespoons butter in a heavy skillet over low heat until butter is just beginning to turn a light brown, but do not allow butter to burn. Stir in pepper and lemon juice. Drizzle over trout. Sprinkle with minced parsley and serve.

Yield: 4 servings

SNAPPER WITH OLIVE SPREAD

OLIVE SPREAD

8   tablespoons (1 stick) butter
2   tablespoons chopped fresh parsley
4   teaspoons fresh lemon juice
¼   cup coarsely chopped green olives with pimiento

FISH

Oil for lubricating fish and greasing grill
2   pounds fresh red snapper fillets, cut into 4-inch-long pieces

   1. *Make Olive Spread:* Place butter in a small saucepan and melt over low heat. Stir in parsley, lemon juice, and olives. Mix well and transfer to serving bowl.
   2. *Grill snapper:* Oil snapper fillet pieces on both sides, then place on oiled grill. Cook for 3–4 minutes on each side or until fish just begins to flake with fork. Remove from heat immediately.
   3. Divide fish pieces evenly among 4 heated dinner plates. Spoon small amount of olive spread over each serving. Serve immediately.

Yield: 4 servings

If you're in a pinch for time and can't remember anything else, remember chive butter. Stir dried chives into soft butter. Serve it with a piece of hot, fresh, grilled fish, some warm French bread, and a hot cooked veggie such as green beans—you need some color on the plate. Your guests can put the chive butter on the fish, the bread, and the green beans. It tastes wonderful.

PART II
THE RECIPES

BLUEFISH

This fish has a delicate yet distinctive flavor. When bluefish is not available, substitute mackerel or whitefish. *

BLUEFISH WITH TOMATO BUTTER

TOMATO BUTTER
3   shallots, minced
1   tablespoon tomato paste
3   tablespoons water
3   tablespoons wine vinegar
16 tablespoons (2 sticks) butter, cut into small pieces
2   teaspoons crumbled dried oregano
1   teaspoon fresh lemon juice
Salt and white pepper to taste

FISH
4   7-ounce bluefish fillets or whole cleaned mackerel, split in half
Crumbled dried oregano to taste
Oil for greasing grill

    1. *Make Tomato Butter:* Mix shallots, tomato paste, water, and wine vinegar in a saucepan. Reduce mixture by cooking over medium heat until approximately 2–3 tablespoons of liquid remain. Whisk in butter, 2 pieces at a time. Mix in oregano and lemon juice. Season tomato butter to taste with salt and white pepper. Refrigerate until ready to serve.

    2. *Grill bluefish:* Sprinkle bluefish with oregano to taste. Place fish on oiled grill and cook for 4–5 minutes. Turn fish over and continue cooking 2 minutes or until fish begins to flake when tested with a fork. Place on individual serving plates and serve with Tomato Butter.

Yield: 4 servings

    *Note: Here and in other fish specie descriptions, a few suggested substitutions are supplied. For a complete breakdown of easily interchanged fish, see chart on pages 12–13.

BUFFALOFISH

This lake fish has a distinctive flavor. When it is not available, substitute snapper.

BUFFALOFISH STUFFED WITH PECANS AND SHERRY

The accompanying recipe for Chunky Applesauce provides the perfect complement for this firm, hearty fish.

STUFFING
2   tablespoons butter
4   ounces fresh mushrooms, chopped
¼   cup finely chopped onion
¼   teaspoon each: salt, pepper, dried thyme, and celery seed
⅛   teaspoon each: ground nutmeg, and ground mace
¾   cup chopped pecans
2¼ cups toasted bread crumbs
3   tablespoons dry sherry

FISH
1   3-pound whole buffalofish, scaled and boned
Oil for lubricating fish and greasing fish basket
4   lemon slices

   1. *Make stuffing:* Melt butter in large frying pan. Add mushrooms and onion and sauté over low heat, stirring often, for about 10–15 minutes or until the liquid has evaporated.
   2. Add salt, pepper, thyme, celery seed, nutmeg, and mace. Continue cooking another moment.
   3. Remove from heat. Stir in pecans, bread crumbs, and sherry. Mix well.
   4. Lightly pack stuffing into cavity of fish.
   5. Oil outside of fish on both sides. Then oil inside of fish basket. Lay 2 slices of lemon on bottom of fish grill basket. Lay

30

fish over lemon slices. Top with 2 additional lemon slices. Attach top of basket.

6. *Grill buffalofish:* Grill stuffed fish about 10 minutes on each side or until fish flakes easily with a fork and outside is beginning to be crispy and brown. Transfer to serving platter. Serve immediately with Homemade Chunky Applesauce.

Yield: 4 servings

HOMEMADE CHUNKY APPLESAUCE

⅓ cup butter
1–2 tablespoons sugar
3 pounds apples, peeled, cored, and chopped
1½ cups dry white wine
2 teaspoons grated lemon zest
½ teaspoon ground cinnamon

1. Melt butter over medium heat in a large saucepan. Add 1 tablespoon sugar and the apples, dry white wine, lemon zest, and cinnamon.

2. Reduce heat to low and simmer apples until most of the liquid has evaporated and apples are very soft but have not yet lost their shape.

3. Taste for sugar and add another tablespoon if desired.

4. Serve hot with Buffalofish Stuffed with Pecans and Sherry.

Yield: about 4–5 cups

CATFISH

A sweet, medium-firm freshwater fish. Substitute orange roughy or walleye pike when catfish is tough to find.

CATFISH WITH CREOLE SAUCE

It's hard to beat catfish, Creole sauce, and hush puppies for a real Southern treat.

CREOLE SAUCE
2   tablespoons butter
1   large clove garlic, minced
1   large onion, minced
2   stalks celery, chopped
1   medium green bell pepper, seeded and chopped
1   bay leaf
½   teaspoon paprika
3   cups peeled, diced fresh or canned tomatoes
½   cup chili sauce

FISH
4   7-ounce catfish fillets
Peanut oil for lubricating fish and greasing grill
½   teaspoon garlic powder
1   teaspoon paprika
Pepper to taste
½   teaspoon crumbled dried tarragon

1. *Make sauce:* Heat butter in medium saucepan and add garlic, onion, celery, and bell pepper. Sauté for 3–5 minutes, stirring often, until vegetables are tender.

2. Add remaining sauce ingredients. Simmer, uncovered, stirring occasionally, for 20 minutes.

3. Remove and discard bay leaf. Place cooled sauce in a

covered container and store in refrigerator until ready to use. Reheat before serving.

4. *Grill catfish.* Brush catfish fillets with oil and sprinkle with seasonings. Arrange fish on prepared grill. Cook for 3 minutes, brush with oil, and turn. Continue cooking until fish begins to flake easily when tested with a fork, 2–4 minutes, depending on the size of the fish.

5. Arrange catfish on heated platter. Pass heated Creole Sauce at table with catfish. Serve with Hush Puppies.

Yield: 4 servings

HUSH PUPPIES

1½ cups yellow cornmeal
½   cup all-purpose flour
2   tablespoons double-acting baking powder
½   teaspoon baking soda
¼   teaspoon salt
1   egg, slightly beaten
1   cup buttermilk
4   tablespoons bacon drippings, melted
2   green onions, minced
2   cups peanut oil

Combine all ingredients except oil in a deep mixing bowl. Let batter stand for 10 minutes at room temperature and stir. Heat oil to 375°F in heavy skillet. Gently slide batter a teaspoonful at a time, into hot oil. Cook about 6 hush puppies at a time. Fry until hush puppies are golden brown on all sides. Drain on paper toweling. Serve hot with Catfish with Creole Sauce.

Yield: 4 servings

CATFISH STUFFED WITH WALNUTS

STUFFING

2   tablespoons butter
½   cup finely chopped onion
½   teaspoon finely chopped fresh hot pepper
¼   teaspoon salt
3   pinches dried rosemary
2   pinches dried thyme
1   cup each: chopped walnuts and bread crumbs

FISH

1   3-pound farm-raised catfish, scaled, boned, head cut off
Oil for lubricating fish and greasing fish basket
4   lemon slices

1. *Make stuffing:* Melt butter in a medium frying pan, add onion and pepper, and sauté 10 minutes or until onion is translucent.

2. Add salt, rosemary, and thyme and mix well over low heat for a moment. Remove from heat and combine with walnuts and bread crumbs, mixing well.

3. Fill catfish cavity with stuffing.

4. Oil catfish on both sides. Oil fish basket. Lay 2 slices of lemon in middle of fish basket. Then arrange catfish so it is lying on lemon slices. Top with 2 more lemon slices, then fasten top of grill basket over fish.

5. Grill over ashen coals. Grill 6–7 minutes on each side or until fish flakes easily when tested with a fork. Serve immediately.

Yield: 4 servings

COD

Cod has a low fat content and a delicate flavor; scrod or flounder
will do in its stead.

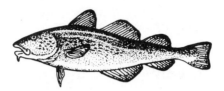

COD WITH SPANISH ALMOND-GARLIC SAUCE

ALMOND-GARLIC SAUCE
2   tablespoons oil
½   cup finely chopped onion
1–2 fresh hot peppers, seeds removed, chopped fine
5   cloves garlic, chopped fine
4   tomatoes, peeled, seeded, and chopped fine
22   whole blanched almonds
½   teaspoon salt
½   cup finely chopped fresh parsley

FISH
Oil for lubricating fish and for greasing grill
2   pounds fresh cod fillets

1. *Make sauce:* Heat 2 tablespoons oil in large saucepan. Sauté
onion and peppers in oil over medium heat for 10 minutes. Add
garlic and cook for an additional 1–2 minutes, taking care that it
doesn't burn. Add tomatoes, heat to simmer, and let cook for 3–4
minutes.
2. Meanwhile, spread almonds on small cookie sheet or
baking dish in a single layer. Place in a 350°F oven for 10 minutes
or until lightly browned. Grind in blender until coarsely grated.
3. Add grated almonds to sauce along with salt. Stir well.
Then remove from heat and stir in parsley.
4. *Grill cod:* Lightly oil cod fillets on both sides. Place on
greased grill over ashen coals. Cook 4–5 minutes on both sides or
until fish just turns white. Transfer cod to heated serving platter.
Spoon sauce over cod. Serve immediately.

Yield: 4 servings

SKEWERED COD WITH GREEK SKORDALIA SAUCE

This smooth, creamy white Greek sauce takes only minutes to make and is delicious with any kind of fresh grilled fish. The garlic flavor is very delicate.

SKORDALIA SAUCE

15 slices white bread, crusts removed
¾ cup hot water
5 medium-size garlic cloves, peeled
¾ cup olive oil
½ cup white wine vinegar
1 squeeze from a lemon half

FISH

2 pounds fresh cod, skinned and boned
Oil for greasing grill
½ cup freshly toasted pine nuts or sliced almonds (optional) for garnish

   1. *Make sauce:* Put bread in food processor container and pour hot water over top to soften. Allow to sit for a moment.
   2. Add garlic, olive oil, wine vinegar, and the squeeze of fresh lemon juice.
   3. Turn on food processor and process for a few moments or until well blended. Sauce should be very smooth.
   4. Cut cod into large squares, about 1¼–1½ inches. Thread onto 4 10″ skewers and arrange skewers in a dish with raised sides. Spoon half of sauce over fish and let sit for 30 minutes, covered, in the refrigerator. Transfer remaining half of sauce to serving dish.
   5. *Grill cod:* Grill kabobs on greased grill over ashen coals turning every 3 minutes until done.
   6. Transfer to serving dish and bring to table. Serve immediately, passing extra sauce and toasted nuts for garnish if desired.

Yield: 4 servings

CRAB

Yes, crab can be grilled! Watch for the reddish color as a
doneness test.

SOFT-SHELLED CRAB WITH GARLIC BUTTER

8   soft-shelled crabs
¼   cup clarified butter (see recipe, Chapter 4)
2   cloves garlic, minced
Salt, pepper, and paprika to taste

    1. To clean soft-shelled crabs, put the crabs, one at a time, on cutting surface. Cut off face portion of crab. Lifting the shell easily on either side of back, scrape off the gills. Lift shell and remove sand receptacle from under the mouth area. Discard all removed portions from the crab. Wash crab and pat dry with paper toweling. (If you make friends with your fishmonger, he may clean them for you.)

    2. Lay each crab on a square of aluminum foil. Begin to fold foil, envelope style, but do not seal.

    3. Heat butter in small saucepan over medium heat. Sauté garlic in it until tender, stirring often.

    4. Drizzle garlic butter over crabs. Sprinkle crabs with salt, pepper, and paprika to taste. Fold and seal envelopes securely.

    5. Arrange crab packages over hot grill in a single layer. Cook for 4–5 minutes. Open one envelope and check to see if crab has steamed (crabs will turn a reddish color when done). If not, rewrap and continue grilling until crabs have cooked. Serve soft-shelled crabs on individual plates, allowing guests to open packages themselves.

Yield: 4 servings

GROUPER

Grouper, a firm fish, can be substituted with all snappers.

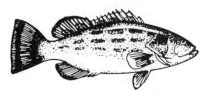

GROUPER WITH SWEET AND SOUR SAUCE

SWEET AND SOUR SAUCE
1   tablespoon cornstarch
½   cup firmly packed dark brown sugar
⅓   cup red wine vinegar
6   tablespoons pineapple juice, reserved from canned pineapple
2   teaspoons soy sauce
1   20-ounce can pineapple chunks, drained, juice reserved
1   green bell pepper, seeded and cut into 1-inch cubes

FISH
4   7-ounce grouper fillets
Peanut oil for lubricating fish and greasing grill
Garlic powder
Sesame seeds for garnish

1. *Make sauce:* Combine cornstarch and brown sugar in a small saucepan. Mix in remaining ingredients except pineapple and pepper. Bring sauce to a boil over medium heat. Reduce heat to a simmer and continue cooking for 1½ minutes, stirring constantly. Mix in pineapple chunks and pepper cubes. Remove sauce from heat. Reheat sauce when ready to serve.

2. *Grill grouper:* Brush grouper fillets with peanut oil and sprinkle with garlic powder. Arrange fillets on prepared grill and cook for 4 minutes. Turn fish over and continue cooking about 2 minutes or until fish begins to flake when tested.

3. Place grouper on a serving platter and drizzle with warm Sweet and Sour Sauce. Sprinkle with sesame seeds; serve with rice.

Yield: 4 servings

HALIBUT
A sweet-flavored fish with a moderately high fat content.

HALIBUT STEAKS WITH TOMATO-BASIL SAUCE

This is a delightful fall recipe, when fresh basil is abundant. Sauce can be made a day or two in advance, making this a potentially no-time-needed recipe.

TOMATO-BASIL SAUCE
2   tablespoons olive oil
1   clove garlic, minced
1   medium onion, minced
2½ cups peeled, diced fresh tomatoes
¼   teaspoon each: salt and freshly ground pepper
3   tablespoons finely chopped fresh basil

FISH
4   7-ounce halibut steaks
Melted butter
Freshly ground white pepper
1   teaspoon crumbled dried basil
Oil for greasing grill

    1. *Make sauce:* Heat oil in saucepan and add garlic and onion. Sauté for 3 minutes, stirring often, until vegetables are tender. Add remaining sauce ingredients. Simmer, uncovered, stirring occasionally, for 10 minutes. Place cooled sauce in covered container and store in refrigerator until ready to use.
    2. *Grill halibut steaks:* Brush halibut steaks with butter and sprinkle steaks with white pepper and basil. Place halibut steaks on prepared grill and cook for 4–5 minutes. Brush fish again, turn, and continue cooking 2–3 minutes until halibut begins to flake when tested. Arrange on individual plates. Reheat sauce and pass at the table.

Yield: 4 servings

HALIBUT CURRY WITH CHUTNEY

This dish is extra delicious with the chutney. Make a double batch of the chutney and give it as your next gift to the host and hostess.

CHUTNEY
2   cups dried apricots
1½ tablespoons chopped candied ginger
1   cup dark raisins
½   lime, sliced thin
1   large onion, sliced thin
1½ cups firmly packed dark brown sugar
½   cup wine vinegar
3   cloves garlic, minced
1   teaspoon dry mustard
½   cup canned tomato sauce
½   teaspoon each: ground cinnamon, ground allspice, and ground cloves

FISH
Curry powder
¼   cup melted butter
4   7-ounce halibut steaks
Oil for greasing grill

    1. *Make chutney:* Wash and chop apricots. Combine all chutney ingredients in a medium-sized heavy saucepan. Simmer for 25 minutes, stirring often, until mixture blends together and has a thick consistency. Pour the cooled chutney into a covered container and refrigerate until ready to serve.
    2. *Grill halibut steaks:* Mix curry powder to taste with melted butter. Brush halibut with curry-butter mixture. Cook steaks on prepared grill for 4–5 minutes. Turn halibut with a greased spatula and continue cooking until fish begins to flake, 2–3 minutes. Remove fish to individual plates. Pass chutney at the table as a sauce for the halibut. Serve with warm Chapatis.

Yield: 4 servings

CHAPATIS (GRILLED INDIAN BREAD)

2   cups whole wheat flour
½   teaspoon salt
2   tablespoons melted butter
¾   cup lukewarm water
Additional melted butter or ghee (clarified butter; see recipe,
    Chapter 4)

1. Place flour and salt in a deep mixing bowl. Mix in melted butter and enough lukewarm water to form a dough. Dough should not be sticky. Form dough into a ball, cover with aluminum foil, and let stand for 1 hour.

2. Divide dough into 12 balls. Roll each into 4–5-inch circle on a lightly floured pastry cloth. Layer dough circles between sheets of aluminum foil and seal with additional foil until ready to grill.

3. Put chapatis, one at a time, on a hot grill surface that has not been greased. Dough will blister. Press edges with a spatula toward the center to help the center of the bread puff. When puffed, turn over and rotate gently. Cook until bread is a pale golden. Remove from grill and brush with a little butter or ghee. Keep warm, covered with foil. Serve with Halibut Curry with Chutney.

Yield: 12 chapatis

LOBSTER

The lobster is a crustacean of the northern hemisphere. Usually, one should bring them home alive from the market. In our recipe we use lobster tails and they are supplied frozen.

ROCK LOBSTER TAILS WITH PERNOD BUTTER

If the solid Pernod butter is served at room temperature, it will melt into the hot lobster immediately.

PERNOD BUTTER
8   tablespoons (1 stick) butter, room temperature
2   tablespoons Pernod liqueur, or to taste
2   teaspoons dried crumbled tarragon

LOBSTER
4   7–8-ounce rock lobster tails, defrosted
Melted butter
Oil for greasing grill

1. *Make Pernod Butter:* Combine 8 tablespoons butter with Pernod and tarragon. Beat until fluffy. Cover and refrigerate until ready to serve.
2. *Grill lobster tails:* With kitchen shears, cut top membrane and discard. Partially loosen meat from shell with your hand, leaving tail section connected. Brush lobster tails with melted butter.
3. Arrange tails on prepared grill, cut side down, and cook for 2–3 minutes. Turn tails over and continue cooking until done, 7–9 minutes. (Grilling lobster shell side down for most of the cooking time helps the lobster meat retain its juices.) The lobster meat is cooked when it turns opaque. The shell may char. Serve lobster tails immediately with Pernod Butter (don't melt the butter; the heat of the lobster will melt it for you) and a large mixed salad.

Yield: 4 servings

MACKEREL

This Atlantic fish has a distinctive flavor and a high fat content; it is similar to bluefish. Butterflied mackerel will cook quickly on a hot grill; consider it when you need to cook in a hurry.

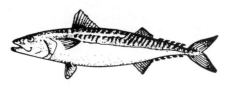

MACKEREL WITH GARLIC AND TOMATOES

Roasting garlic on the grill transforms the flavor from pungent to mellow. Soft, roasted cloves can actually be squeezed out and spread onto toasted French bread.

4   large fresh tomatoes, peeled and chopped
½   teaspoon crumbled dried oregano
Salt and pepper to taste
1   head garlic with large cloves
2   mackerel, about 1½ pounds each, cleaned and split in half
Crumbled dried rosemary
Oil for greasing grill

1. Toss tomatoes with oregano, salt, and pepper. Set aside.
2. Loosen unpeeled cloves of garlic and place on grill at edge of hot coals about 10–15 minutes before starting to grill fish.
3. Sprinkle mackerel with rosemary. Arrange fish on prepared grill or in an oiled double-hinged grill basket. Secure basket. Sprinkle 2 tablespoons rosemary over hot coals. Grill mackerel for 3 minutes, turn fish over, and continue cooking about 3 minutes, or until fish begins to flake when tested. Turn garlic occasionally as you are grilling the mackerel. Roast garlic for 20 minutes altogether, or until the insides of the cloves are soft. Place mackerel on heated platter. Arrange tomato mixture around grilled fish. Separate garlic cloves and sprinkle over fish. Garlic, when grilled, has a mild, somewhat nutty taste. Serve fish and allow guests to squeeze out the garlic from individual cloves and spread over mackerel.

Yield: 4 servings

MAHIMAHI

Mahimahi is a medium-textured fish with a high fat content.
Substitute snapper, yellowtail, and sea trout.

MAHIMAHI WITH ALMONDS

The cilantro, singed in the basket, will still be tasty when brought to the table.

¾ cup cilantro (coriander) sprigs
Peanut oil for greasing fish basket
3 oranges, sliced thin
4 7-ounce mahimahi fillets
2 cloves garlic, minced
½ cup sliced almonds

Arrange half of the cilantro sprigs over prepared double-hinged fish basket. Put orange slices over cilantro and top with mahimahi. Sprinkle fish with garlic and remaining cilantro. Secure basket. Grill mahimahi with orange and cilantro in place for 4–5 minutes. Turn grill basket over and continue cooking 2–3 minutes or until fish begins to flake when tested with a fork. Put fish on individual plates and sprinkle with sliced almonds.

Serve with corn tortillas warmed in the oven. If you wish, spread mahimahi on the warm tortilla, sprinkle with almonds, roll, and enjoy.

Yield: 4 servings

MAHIMAHI KABOBS WITH FRUIT

Kabobs should be turned every 3 minutes to ensure even cooking; remember, any firm-fleshed fish can make a delicious kabob.

2　cups fresh or canned pineapple chunks, drained
3　bananas, peeled and cut into 2-inch chunks
1½ pounds mahimahi fillets, cut into 1½-inch pieces
2　limes, sliced
4　tablespoons (½ stick) butter
4　tablespoons light brown sugar
Oil for greasing grill
Freshly grated coconut

    1. Thread fruit, mahimahi pieces, and lime slices alternately on 4 10-inch skewers.
    2. Melt butter with brown sugar in a saucepan.
    3. Brush kabobs with sugar-butter mixture and arrange kabobs on prepared grill. Cook for 3 minutes, turn, and rotate kabobs every 3 minutes until mahimahi begins to flake when tested with a fork.
    4. Arrange on individual plates and sprinkle with coconut. Allow guest to remove fish and fruit from skewers.

Yield: 4 servings

ONO
Ono is a Pacific fish that can be substituted with swordfish.

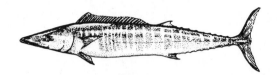

ONO STEAKS WITH GRILLED PINEAPPLE

Delicious served with corn on the grill.

PINEAPPLE SAUCE
Reserved pineapple juice
Extra pineapple juice
1½ tablespoons cornstarch, mixed with 2 tablespoons pineapple
    juice
¼ teaspoon each: ground cumin and ground ginger

MARINADE
¼ cup pineapple juice
2 tablespoons fresh orange juice
4 tablespoons soy sauce
3 tablespoons chili sauce

FISH
4 7-ounce ono or shark steaks
1 5¼-ounce can pineapple slices, juice reserved, or 1 fresh
    pineapple, pared and cut into 1½-inch slices
Oil for greasing grill
White pepper
1 teaspoon minced garlic

1. *Make sauce:* Measure reserved pineapple juice and add enough extra juice to measure 1½ cups. In a small saucepan, combine juice and remaining sauce ingredients. Cook over medium heat, stirring often, until sauce thickens slightly. Remove pan from heat. Reheat sauce when ready to serve.

2. *Marinate ono steaks:* Combine marinade ingredients in a shallow glass bowl or pie plate. Marinate fish in mixture for 1 hour, turning once. Drain, reserving extra marinade.

3. *Grill ono steaks:* Arrange steaks on prepared grill, sprinkle with garlic and pepper to taste, and cook for 4 minutes. Grill pineapple slices 3–5 minutes on each side and reserve. Brush ono steaks with reserved marinade and turn fish. Continue grilling for 2–3 minutes, depending on the thickness of fish, until fish begins to flake when tested with a fork.

4. Place fish on heated platter and drizzle with sauce. Place grilled pineapple around fish.

Yield: 4 servings

CORN ON THE GRILL

6   ears corn, husks left on
Butter
Salt and pepper to taste

1. Gently pull back husks over each corn ear without breaking off. Remove and discard the silk. Replace the husks. Soak corn in cold water for 25–30 minutes before grilling.

2. Drain corn. Pull back husks again and rub corn with butter. Replace husks over corn.

3. Place corn on prepared grill and cook for 12–15 minutes, turning every 5 minutes.

4. Remove and discard husks. Place corn on individual plates and serve with butter, salt, and pepper.

Yield: 4 servings

ORANGE ROUGHY

Orange Roughy is a very mild, delicate fish; sole or turbot would also work well in orange roughy recipes.

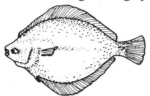

ORANGE ROUGHY FILLETS ON A BED OF SAUTEED GREEN ONIONS

The slightly tangy taste of the cole slaw marries well with the delicate, light taste of orange roughy.

3   tablespoons butter
2   cloves garlic, minced
1   bunch green onions, trimmed and cut into 2-inch pieces
½   teaspoon crumbled dried chervil
4   7-ounce orange roughy fillets
Melted butter
Oil for greasing fish basket
1   tablespoon capers, drained, for garnish

1. While coals are heating, prepare green onions. Melt butter in skillet. Sauté garlic in it until soft. Add green onions and chervil and sauté until tender, stirring occasionally. Arrange onions in a nest design on a serving platter.

2. Brush roughy fillets with butter. Arrange in a prepared fish basket and grill for 2–4 minutes. Turn fish and continue grilling for about 3 minutes, depending on the thickness of the fish, until fish begins to flake when tested with a fork. Place fish over green onions and sprinkle with capers. Serve with Creamy Cole Slaw.

Yield: 4 servings

CREAMY COLE SLAW

1   medium-large head cabbage, cored
1   medium onion, chopped
1   large carrot, grated
¾ cup mayonnaise
¼ cup dairy sour cream
3   tablespoons red wine vinegar
2   tablespoons sugar
2   teaspoons caraway seeds
Salt and pepper to taste

    1. Finely grate cabbage and place in large mixing bowl. Mix in onion and carrot.
    2. In a small bowl, combine mayonnaise, sour cream, vinegar, sugar, and caraway seeds.
    3. Toss dressing with cabbage. Season cole slaw with salt and pepper. Chill thoroughly before serving. Serve with Orange Roughy Fillets on a Bed of Sautéed Green Onions.

Yield: 8 servings

OYSTERS

According to old wives' tales, one should only eat oysters in months that contain an *r*. Due to modern methods in transportation, refrigeration, and aquaculture (oyster farming) you can now enjoy them all year long. Oysters can be eaten raw or cooked. They are always cooked lightly (only on the outside) and should be juicy and plump.

OYSTERS EN BROCHETTE

Oysters are elegant—but kabobs are versatile. Shrimp, salmon chunks, swordfish, and many other firm-fleshed seafood would be delightful in this recipe.

8 slices lean bacon, cut in half widthwise, partially cooked, and drained
16 medium-large fresh mushroom caps
3 dozen oysters, shucked
1 large red onion, cut into quarters, sections loosened
2 large firm fresh tomatoes, cut into quarters
Salt and pepper to taste
Oil for greasing grill

   1. Wrap a bacon strip securely around each mushroom. Thread 4 10″ skewers alternately with oysters, vegetables, and bacon-wrapped mushroom caps. Add extra oysters as you thread. Sprinkle with salt and pepper to taste.
   2. Arrange skewers on oiled grill in single layer and grill for 3 minutes on each side or until cooked. Place skewers on individual plates and allow guests to remove food themselves.

Yield: 4 servings

*Oysters en Brochette, page 50; Salmon steaks sprinkled
with fennel seeds and dill weed while grilling;
mackerel grilled with lime.*

Orange Roughy Fillets on a Bed of Sautéed Green Onions (en croute), page 48. Below: Orange Roughy, grilling on a hibachi.

Rock Lobster Tails with Pernod Butter, page 42; Creamy Cole Slaw, page 49; Corn on the Grill, page 47.

Mackerel with Garlic and Tomatoes, page 43.

PIKE

A medium-firm freshwater fish that can be substituted with flounder or rainbow trout.

PIKE FILLETS IN GRAPE LEAVES

This beautiful dish would make a sensational centerpiece—but it never seems to last long enough to get a good look.

1   9-ounce jar grape leaves, washed and drained
4   7-ounce pike fillets
Olive oil for lubricating fish and greasing fish basket
Minced fresh parsley and chives
1   lemon, sliced, for garnish
Greek olives for garnish

    1. Layer grape leaves, dull side up, on the bottom of a prepared double-hinged fish basket. Arrange pike fillets over leaves. Brush with olive oil. Sprinkle with parsley and chives. Cover with a layer of grape leaves and secure basket.
    2. Grill 7–10 minutes and turn basket over. Continue grilling about 3 minutes or until fish begins to flake when tested with a fork. Remove fish and grape leaves to individual serving dishes. Serve with lemon slices and sprinkle with Greek olives.

Yield: 4 servings

POMPANO

A medium-textured fish with a high fat content. When pompano is not available, ono or swordfish will do.

POMPANO IN FOIL PACKETS

3 tablespoons butter
3 large shallots, peeled and minced
½ pound mushrooms, minced
4 5- to 6-ounce pompano fillets
¼ teaspoon each: salt and white pepper
4 large mushrooms, sliced

　　1. Melt butter in medium skillet; sauté shallots and mushrooms in butter until vegetables are tender and dry. Reserve.
　　2. Cut 4 sheets of aluminum foil, each twice the size of a fish fillet. Arrange a piece of fish on each sheet of foil. Season with salt and pepper. Distribute the mushroom mixture over the fish. Arrange a sliced mushroom decoratively over each piece of fish. Fold foil envelope style.
　　3. Arrange fish packages over hot grill in single layer. Grill for 10–15 minutes and check one envelope to see if the fish has cooked. If not, rewrap and continue grilling until cooked. Serve pompano packages on individual plates, allowing guests to open packages themselves.

Yield: 4 servings

REDFISH

A mild-flavored fish with a low fat content. When redfish is not available substitute black bass, halibut, or bluefish (fillets).

BLACKENED REDFISH

This popular dish is started indoors. If you wish, cook it indoors an hour before your guests arrive, then finish it on the grill.

4   7-ounce redfish or bluefish fillets
½   cup melted butter
1   tablespoon paprika
½   teaspoon each: salt, freshly ground black pepper, and freshly ground white pepper
1   teaspoon dried minced onion
½   teaspoon crumbled dried thyme
¼   teaspoon garlic powder

1. Rinse fish and pat dry with paper toweling. Place a large cast iron skillet over high heat on stove and allow it to preheat 3–4 minutes. (Open kitchen windows as the high heat will cause a great deal of smoke. Use proper ventilation.) Brush fish fillets with melted butter. Combine remaining ingredients and sprinkle both sides of fish with spice mixture.

2. Carefully place the redfish, one piece at a time, in the dry hot skillet. Drizzle 3 tablespoons of the melted butter over fish. Sear fish 30 seconds on each side, turning with a spatula.

3. Using a pot holder, carry skillet outdoors and place on prepared hot grill. Continue cooking, turning fish every minute, for about 3–4 minutes, depending on thickness of fish, until it cooks and is darkened. Add more butter as necessary. To serve, remove redfish to individual plates and drizzle with remaining melted butter. Serve with cornbread.

Yield: 4 servings

REDFISH WITH CREOLE-CHORON SAUCE

CHORON SAUCE
¼ cup Creole Sauce (see recipe on page 32)
½ cup Béarnaise Sauce (see recipe)

FISH
4   7-ounce redfish, sea trout, or grouper fillets
Melted butter
Pepper to taste
Oil for greasing grill
Tomato slices for garnish
Fresh tarragon leaves for garnish

1. *Make sauce:* Heat Creole Sauce in small saucepan over medium-low heat until sauce is reduced by half. Whisk in Béarnaise Sauce and continue cooking until sauce is combined and heated, about 1 minute. Set aside and reheat before serving.

2. *Grill redfish:* Brush redfish fillets with butter and season with pepper to taste. Arrange fish on prepared grill and cook for 5 minutes. Brush fish with melted butter and turn fish over. Continue cooking until fish begins to flake easily when tested with a fork, about 5 minutes.

3. Transfer fish to warm serving platter. Ladle sauce over fish and surround platter with tomato slices sprinkled with chopped tarragon leaves. Ladle warm sauce over fish and serve immediately.

Yield: 4 servings

BEARNAISE SAUCE

¼   cup tarragon vinegar or red wine vinegar
¼   cup dry white wine
1   large shallot, peeled and minced
¼   teaspoon pepper
4   egg yolks, room temperature
1   cup (2 sticks) butter, cut in ½-inch pieces
1   teaspoon crumbled dried tarragon leaves
¼   teaspoon salt
1   teaspoon fresh lemon juice

In a heavy nonaluminum saucepan, combine vinegar, wine, shallot, and pepper. Cook over medium heat until mixture is reduced to only 2 tablespoons. Remove pan from heat and whisk in the egg yolks, one at a time. Place mixture in top of a double boiler over simmering water. Whisk butter into sauce, one piece at a time, until all the butter has been incorporated. Mix in tarragon, salt, and lemon juice. Keep sauce warm over a pan of hot, but not boiling, water. The sauce should be served warm or at room temperature.

Yield: 1½ cups sauce

RED SEA BASS

A firm fish with a mild flavor and low fat content. Redfish, striped sea bass, or monkfish will work in red sea bass recipes.

RED SEA BASS IN A JAPANESE MARINADE

2   pounds red sea bass, cut into 4-inch-long fillets, skin on
1   teaspoon finely chopped fresh gingerroot
¾   teaspoon finely chopped garlic
¼   cup each: soy sauce, water, and sherry
2   teaspoons sugar
Oil for greasing grill

1. Lay fish in dish with raised sides.
2. In a separate bowl, mix gingerroot, garlic, soy sauce, water, sherry, and sugar.
3. Pour over fish, cover with plastic wrap, and refrigerate for 30 minutes.
4. Put fillets on well-greased grill, skin side down, over ashen coals. Grill on one side only. Brush leftover marinade on fish 2 or 3 times during grilling. Serve immediately.

Yield: 4 servings

RED SEA BASS WITH REMOULADE SAUCE

REMOULADE SAUCE

3   egg yolks
¾   cup vegetable oil
2   tablespoons chopped fresh parsley
2   cloves garlic
2   green onions, cut into 1-inch pieces
1   teaspoon paprika
Dash Tabasco sauce, or to taste

FISH

4   7-ounce red sea bass, sea trout, or grouper fillets
Melted butter
White pepper to taste
Oil for greasing grill

    1. *Make sauce:* Using a food processor fitted with steel blade or a blender, process egg yolks until light. With machine running, pour oil through feed tube in a slow, steady stream until it is incorporated. Add remaining sauce ingredients and puree. Place sauce in a covered container and refrigerate until ready to serve.

    2. *Grill bass:* Brush bass fillets with butter and sprinkle with pepper to taste. Place fish on prepared grill and cook for 4 minutes. Check fish and continue cooking about 2–3 minutes or until it begins to flake easily when tested with a fork. Place fish on individual plates. Ladle sauce over bass and serve.

Yield: 4 servings

RED SNAPPER

This is a medium-firm fish with a mild flavor. All snappers are interchangeable in recipes; halibut will work as well.

INDIVIDUAL RED SNAPPERS

4 small red snappers, about 8–10 ounces each, cleaned, head
    and tail intact
Italian salad dressing
Freshly ground pepper
Crumbled dried oregano
Freshly grated Parmesan cheese
Oil for greasing grill
Pretty Romaine lettuce leaves for garnish
Watercress for garnish
Black olives for garnish

1. Brush snappers with salad dressing and sprinkle with pepper, oregano, and Parmesan cheese.
2. Arrange fish on prepared grill. Cook fish about 4 minutes. Brush with salad dressing and turn, using a spatula. Continue grilling about 2–3 minutes, until fish begins to flake when tested with a fork.
3. Place Romaine lettuce leaves on a serving platter. Arrange snappers over lettuce and garnish with watercress and black olives.

Yield: 4 servings

RED SNAPPER FILLETS WITH BEURRE ROUGE SAUCE

BEURRE ROUGE SAUCE

3   large shallots, minced
1   cup dry red wine
2   tablespoons wine vinegar
16 tablespoons (2 sticks) butter, room temperature, cut into
     ½-inch pieces

FISH

4   7-ounce red snapper or grouper fillets
Melted butter
Oil for greasing grill

1. *Make sauce:* Combine shallots, wine, and vinegar in a heavy nonaluminum saucepan and reduce mixture until almost evaporated, leaving only 3 tablespoons of liquid. Strain. Remove saucepan from the heat, add 2 pieces of the butter, and whisk until combined. Continue whisking in butter, 2 pieces at a time, being careful not to allow the sauce to separate. If the sauce separates, quickly whisk and try to emulsify. Serve sauce immediately or keep warm in top of a double boiler over simmering water.

2. *Grill red snapper:* Brush red snapper fillets with melted butter. Arrange fish on prepared grill and cook 2–3 minutes, depending on thickness of fish, until fish begins to flake easily when tested with a fork. It is not necessary to turn fillets over. If desired, you can grill snapper fillets in a prepared double-hinged grill basket, turning once. Place red snapper fillets on individual serving dishes and drizzle with Beurre Rouge Sauce.

Yield: 4 servings

RED SNAPPER IN THE STYLE OF VERACRUZ

This recipe is classically served with a tomato sauce, garnished with olives, and served with potatoes. We are sure that you will enjoy this adaptation.

VERACRUZ SAUCE
4   tablespoons vegetable oil
3   cloves garlic, minced
2   medium onions, sliced
4   large fresh tomatoes, peeled and quartered
½   cup sliced green olives
Salt and pepper to taste

FISH
1   2½- to 3-pound whole red snapper fillet
Oil for lubricating fish and greasing grill
Fresh lime juice

   1. *Make sauce:* Heat 4 tablespoons oil in a saucepan; sauté garlic and onions in it until tender, stirring occasionally. Mix in tomatoes and olives and continue cooking over medium heat for 6–8 minutes. Season to taste with salt and pepper. Remove saucepan from heat and reserve. Reheat when ready to serve.
   2. *Grill red snapper:* Brush red snapper with vegetable oil and sprinkle with lime juice, including cavity. Place snapper on prepared grill and cook for 6–10 minutes or use a greased double layer of aluminum foil poked with holes. Brush fish with oil and turn with spatula. Continue cooking 2–3 minutes, depending on the thickness of fish, until the fish begins to flake when tested with fork. Place fish on heated platter and pour heated Veracruz Sauce over top. Serve with boiled new potatoes.

Yield: 4 servings

RED SNAPPER WITH RED SALSA

RED SALSA

2   tablespoons vegetable oil
1   clove garlic, minced
1   medium onion, chopped
2   large tomatoes, peeled and chopped
1   small fresh hot pepper, or to taste (1 pepper gives a sting; 2
    peppers give a bite)
¼   teaspoon each: salt and freshly ground black pepper
3   tablespoons chopped fresh cilantro (coriander)

FISH

¼   cup peanut oil
Juice of 1 lime or lemon
4   7-ounce red snapper fillets
Oil for greasing grill
½   cup whole pitted green olives for garnish

　　1. *Make salsa:* Heat vegetable oil in saucepan and sauté garlic
and onion in it until tender. Add remaining salsa ingredients
except cilantro. Simmer sauce for 10 minutes, stirring
occasionally. Adjust seasonings. Stir in cilantro and continue
cooking 1 minute. Serve salsa hot or cold.
　　2. *Grill red snapper:* Mix peanut oil and lime juice and baste
snapper with mixture. Cook fish on prepared grill for 6 minutes,
baste, and turn snapper. Continue grilling 2–3 minutes, depending
on thickness of fish, until fish begins to flake when tested with a
fork. Place fish on heated platter, garnish with olives, and serve
with spooned salsa over fish and on the side for dipping and fried
corn tortillas.

Yield: 4 servings

RED SNAPPER WITH TWO BUTTERS

GARLIC-CASHEW BUTTER

8 tablespoons (1 stick) butter
1 small clove garlic, minced very fine
2 tablespoons chopped fresh parsley
½ cup finely chopped salted cashews

ROMANO OR PARMESAN CHEESE BUTTER

8 tablespoons (1 stick) butter
½ cup each: freshly grated Romano or Parmesan cheese (do not use pregrated cheese) and finely chopped fresh parsley

FISH

Oil for lubricating fish and greasing grill
2 pounds red snapper fillets, cut into 4-inch-long pieces
4 large sprigs parsley or watercress with stems for garnish

   1. *Make Garlic-Cashew Butter:* Melt 8 tablespoons butter in a small saucepan. Stir in garlic, 2 tablespoons parsley, and chopped cashews. Transfer to serving bowl.
   2. *Make Romano Butter:* Melt 8 tablespoons butter in a small saucepan over low heat. Stir in grated cheese and ½ cup parsley. Transfer to serving bowl.
   3. *Grill red snapper:* Oil red snapper on both sides and place on prepared grill. Cook for just 3 minutes on each side or until fish has turned white.
   4. Divide fish among 4 heated dinner plates, laying fish sections in center. Spoon a little Garlic-Cashew Butter on one side of fish; then spoon a little Romano Butter on other side. Garnish each serving with a parsley sprig. Serve immediately.

Yield: 4 servings

SZECHWAN-STYLE RED SNAPPER FILLETS

SZECHWAN SAUCE

2   tablespoons peanut oil
½   teaspoon minced fresh gingerroot
2   cloves garlic, minced
3   green onions, minced
1–2 fresh chili peppers, chopped (1 pepper gives a sting; 2
      peppers give a bite)
2   tablespoons sugar
5   teaspoons dark soy sauce
3   tablespoons catsup
2   teaspoons dry white wine
1   teaspoon white vinegar
1   tablespoon water
1   teaspoon sesame oil

FISH

4   7-ounce red snapper fillets
Peanut oil for lubricating fish and greasing grill
2   green onions, minced, for garnish

1. *Make sauce:* Heat 2 tablespoons peanut oil over medium heat in a small saucepan. Lightly brown ginger, garlic, onions, and chili pepper in it. Stir-fry as they cook. Stir in remaining sauce ingredients and cook until sauce is heated. Reserve.

2. *Grill red snapper:* Brush red snapper fillets with peanut oil and arrange on prepared grill. Cook for 5–6 minutes. Brush fillets with peanut oil and turn over with a spatula. Continue cooking 2–3 minutes, depending on thickness of the fish, until fish begins to flake when tested with a fork. Place fish on platter and pour heated Szechwan Sauce over top. Sprinkle with green onions and serve with warm Oriental noodles.

Yield: 4 servings

ROCKFISH

This West Coast fish is medium firm with a mild flavor.
Substitute snapper or monkfish when it is not available.

ROCKFISH WITH LEMON SAUCE

Sprinkling rosemary over the hot coals adds a gourmet touch.

LEMON SAUCE
1   clove garlic, minced
Juice of 2 lemons
¼   cup olive oil
¼   teaspoon white pepper
1   teaspoon Dijon mustard
1   tablespoon grated lemon zest

FISH
¼   cup olive oil
2   teaspoons leaf rosemary
¼   teaspoon white pepper
4   7-ounce rockfish fillets
1   lemon, sliced
Oil for greasing fish basket

1. *Make sauce:* Puree all sauce ingredients in a blender or a food processor fitted with a steel blade. Set sauce aside until ready to serve.

2. *Marinate rockfish:* Combine ¼ cup olive oil with 1 teaspoon of the rosemary and the pepper. Brush fillets with seasonings. Let marinate for 1 hour.

3. *Grill rockfish:* Put 1 lemon slice over each piece of fish. Place rockfish in a greased hinged fish basket. Sprinkle remaining rosemary over hot coals. Grill fish for 5 minutes. Turn basket and continue grilling 2–3 minutes, depending on thickness of fish, until fish begins to flake when tested with a fork. Arrange rockfish on individual plates, leaving the lemon slices in place. Drizzle with Lemon Sauce.

Yield: 4 servings

VEGGIES ON THE GRILL: many vegetables can be grilled along with the fish for an easy, thematic meal. Eggplant, pepper strips, onion slices, even carrots and tomatoes can be brushed with oil and grilled. Remember to watch vegetables closely, because they cook quickly. Sprinkle with salt and pepper, if desired, and serve.

SALMON

This popular cold-water fish lends itself easily to grilling. Grouper and monkfish (whether fillets, steaks, or whole fish) can be substituted.

SALMON AU POIVRE WITH LIME

This dish, for those who like "hot" food, can be made even hotter by using more crushed peppercorns. It is adapted from the classic French recipe Steak Au Poivre.

2½ tablespoons peppercorns
2   tablespoons each: melted butter and fresh lime juice
4   salmon steaks, each about 1 inch thick
8   slices fresh lime
Oil for greasing fish basket
Lime wedges for garnish
Tartar Sauce (see index for recipe)

1. Crush peppercorns using mortar and pestle. Or, if no mortar is available, put peppercorns in kitchen towel, then fold it to form envelope. Use a hammer to crush peppercorns coarsely.

2. Combine melted butter and lime juice and brush each salmon steak on one side with the mixture. Press crushed peppercorns thickly into salmon steaks with heel of hand. Turn and brush remaining side with melted butter and lime combination. Press crushed peppercorns thickly into remaining side of salmon steaks.

3. Arrange 4 slices of lime in prepared fish basket and set salmon steaks over lime slices. Top each salmon steak with another lime slice. Fasten top of basket. Grill over ashen coals for about 4 minutes on each side or until fish flakes easily with fork. Serve immediately, garnished with lime wedges.

Note: Lime wedges are important; or substitute homemade Tartar Sauce.

Yield: 4 servings

SALMON FILLETS WITH CHAMPAGNE SAUCE

CHAMPAGNE SAUCE

1   cup chicken stock
½   teaspoon crumbled dried thyme
1   shallot, minced
⅛   teaspoon ground nutmeg
1   cup champagne
1   cup heavy cream
2   tablespoons cold unsalted butter, cut into ½-inch pieces
Salt and white pepper to taste
1   tablespoon champagne vinegar
¼   cup champagne

FISH

4   7-ounce salmon fillets
Melted butter
Oil for greasing grill
Salmon roe for garnish

1. *Make sauce:* Place chicken stock in saucepan; mix in thyme, shallot, nutmeg, and 1 cup champagne. Bring sauce mixture to a boil over medium heat. Continue cooking until mixture is reduced to 2–3 tablespoons. Strain mixture and return to saucepan; stir in heavy cream. Place saucepan over low heat and simmer for 2–4 minutes. Remove from heat. Whisk in butter and season with salt and pepper to taste. Stir in vinegar. Just before serving, whisk in ¼ cup champagne. Serve warm.

2. *Grill salmon:* Brush salmon fillets with melted butter and place on prepared grill. Cook for 4–5 minutes, brush salmon with butter, and turn. Continue cooking 2–3 minutes until fish begins to flake when tested with a fork. Put salmon on individual plates and ladle warm sauce over top. Sprinkle with salmon roe. Serve with a green salad.

Yield: 4 servings

WHOLE SALMON WITH LIME-GINGER CREAM SAUCE

Whole salmon and apple pie is an old New England combination, usually served during the 4th of July celebration. At that time of year beautiful salmon are plentiful.

Even though this dish is not in our 5-minute chapter, it almost could be if simplicity were the only requirement.

LIME-GINGER CREAM SAUCE

6 ounces Neufchâtel cheese, room temperature
½ cup plain yogurt
1 tablespoon chopped candied ginger
Grated zest of 1 lime

FISH

1 3- to 3½-pound whole salmon, cleaned and scaled, head and tail intact
Peanut oil for lubricating fish and greasing grill
Freshly ground pepper to taste
Ground gingerroot
1 lime, sliced

1. *Make sauce:* Mix together cheese, yogurt, ginger, and lime zest in a small bowl. Serve at room temperature over the hot salmon.

2. *Grill salmon:* Brush salmon, including the cavity, with oil. Sprinkle with pepper and ginger. Put sliced lime in the cavity of the salmon. Place fish on prepared grill or over a double thickness on greased aluminum foil with poked holes to allow the smoke to come through. Cook for 10 minutes. Brush salmon with oil and turn with spatula. Continue cooking for 8–10 minutes or until the fish begins to flake when tested with a fork. With a spatula, carefully transfer salmon to serving platter. Serve salmon with Lime-Ginger Cream Sauce, with All-American Apple Pie (recipe follows) for dessert.

Yield: 4–5 servings

ALL-AMERICAN APPLE PIE

PIE CRUST
3   cups all-purpose flour
¼   teaspoon salt
¼   pound (1 stick) butter, cut into small pieces
5   tablespoons vegetable shortening
6–7 tablespoons ice water

FILLING
6   cups cooking apples, peeled and sliced
1   tablespoon fresh lemon juice
1   teaspoon ground cinnamon
¼   teaspoon ground nutmeg
¾   cup sugar
3   tablespoons all-purpose flour
2   tablespoons butter, cut into small pieces
½   cup golden raisins

1. *Make crust:* Place 3 cups flour in a deep bowl and mix in salt. Cut in ¼ pound butter and the shortening with a pastry knife, 2 knives, or a food processor fitted with a steel blade. Add water, a tablespoonful at a time, and mix until pastry holds together. Form dough into a ball. Cover with plastic wrap and chill for 20 minutes. Divide dough in half. Roll out bottom crust on a pastry cloth. Fit the crust into a 9½″ pie plate. Trim edges with a knife.

2. *Make filling:* Preheat oven to 400°F. Toss all filling ingredients in a large mixing bowl. Arrange apple mixture in bottom crust. Roll out remaining crust. Cover pie with top crust and seal edges. Cut ½-inch air vent in center of pie. Bake pie for 15 minutes. Reduce heat to 350°F and continue baking for 20 minutes or until pie is done. Cool pie to room temperature. Serve with sliced cheddar cheese or vanilla ice cream.

Yield: 6–8 servings

SALMON STEAKS WITH FENNEL

Sprinkling fennel on the hot coals will make the fennel aroma delicately flavor the fish.

MARINADE
2 tablespoons minced fresh parsley
2 shallots, minced
1 tablespoon chopped fresh fennel or 1 teaspoon dried fennel seeds
Pepper to taste
¼ cup salad oil
Juice of 2 limes

FISH
4 6- to 7-ounce salmon steaks
1 tablespoon chopped fresh fennel or 1 teaspoon dried fennel seeds
Oil for greasing grill

1. *Marinate salmon steaks:* Combine parsley, shallots, 1 tablespoon fennel, pepper, oil, and lime juice in a shallow glass bowl or pie plate. Place fish in marinade and turn after 30 minutes. Leave fish to marinate for 15 minutes longer.

2. *Grill salmon steaks:* Sprinkle 1 tablespoon of the fennel over hot coals. Place fish on prepared grill and cook for 5 minutes. Brush salmon with remaining marinade and turn. Continue cooking 2–3 minutes, depending on thickness of the fish, until fish begins to flake when tested with a fork. Arrange the fish on individual plates and serve with a mixed salad and thinly sliced white or red onions.

Yield: 4 servings

SCROD

Scrod is a low-fat delicate fish (it's actually young cod or haddock) that can be interchanged with flounder in recipes.

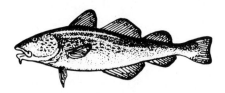

SCROD WITH HOT HORSERADISH-PISTACHIO SAUCE

SAUCE

2 egg yolks
1 cup sour cream, room temperature
2 tablespoons heavy cream
⅓ cup white horseradish
⅛ teaspoon white pepper
1 teaspoon sugar
½ teaspoon salt
1 teaspoon lemon juice

FISH

Oil for lubricating fish and greasing grill
2 pounds scrod fillets
⅓ cup green pistachios, shelled

1. *Make sauce:* Stir egg yolks, sour cream, heavy cream, horseradish, white pepper, sugar, and salt together in small, heavy-bottomed saucepan. Heat slowly over low heat and cook, stirring, for about 5 minutes, or until sauce thickens slightly. Stir in lemon juice.

2. *Grill scrod:* Meanwhile, oil fish fillets on both sides. Place on prepared grill for 3–4 minutes on each side or until fish is just cooked. Transfer fish to serving platter. Top with warm sauce and sprinkle with pistachios.

Yield: 4 servings

SEA SCALLOPS

Scallops are mollusks dredged from the coastal waters. The edible muscle is a round, white, delicate, and delicious food. Sometimes the red roe is available.

SCALLOPS ON A BED OF PEPPERS WITH AVOCADO SAUCE

AVOCADO SAUCE
1   large avocado, peeled and pitted
1   teaspoon fresh lemon juice
2   teaspoons mayonnaise
¼   teaspoon each: salt and cayenne pepper
1   hard-boiled egg, peeled and chopped
1   cup chopped pecans

SCALLOPS
4   tablespoons butter
1   tablespoon olive oil
2   green bell peppers, seeded and sliced thin
2   red bell peppers, seeded and sliced thin
1½ pounds sea scallops
Peanut oil for lubricating scallops and greasing fish basket

1. *Make sauce:* Mash avocado pulp with lemon juice in a mixing bowl. Blend in mayonnaise, salt, cayenne, and egg. Stir in chopped pecans.
2. *Prepare peppers:* Heat butter and olive oil in a large heavy skillet. Sauté pepper slices, stirring often, until tender. Arrange pepper slices on heated serving platter.
3. *Grill scallops:* Place scallops in a greased double-hinged

fish basket. Brush scallops with peanut oil. Grill scallops for 3–4 minutes. Turn basket and continue cooking until scallops begin to turn opaque. Or thread scallops on skewers and turn every 3 minutes until done. Remove scallops and arrange on the bed of peppers. Serve scallops hot and pass Avocado Sauce at the table.

Yield: 4 servings

GARLIC, GREAT ON THE GRILL: garlic on the grill is incomparable. Place a large garlic clove at the outer edges of the coals. Cook, turning occasionally, 15–20 minutes until soft and spreadable. Then, squeeze and spread on french bread, or directly onto the grilled fish. The taste is mild and almost nutty—delectable.

SEAFOOD BROCHETTES WITH CHIVE BUTTER

6   slices bacon
1   pound medium to large raw shrimp, peeled and deveined
1   pound sea scallops
1   pound firm-fleshed fish such as scrod, cut into 1-inch chunks
Cherry tomatoes
Mushroom caps
Melted butter for brushing kabobs
Oil for greasing grill

CHIVE BUTTER
8   tablespoons (1 stick) butter
4   teaspoons snipped fresh chives or more if desired (if
    necessary, substitute frozen or freeze-dried chives)

1. Cook bacon until just done. Drain, pat with paper towels to remove as much fat as possible, and cut into 1½-inch pieces.

2. Thread shrimp, scallops, and scrod chunks onto 4 10" skewers, alternating with bacon pieces, cherry tomatoes, and mushroom caps. Brush with melted butter.

3. *Make Chive Butter:* Melt 8 tablespoons butter with chives. Transfer to small bowl and set aside while skewered fish cooks.

4. *Grill brochettes:* Arrange skewers on well-greased grill over ashen coals. Cook 3–4 minutes on each side or until lightly browned. Serve immediately with bowl of Chive Butter.

Yield: 4 servings

SEA SCALLOPS WITH HOMEMADE TARTAR SAUCE

Be sure to use a grill basket because the scallops could fall through the grill.

TARTAR SAUCE
2 egg yolks, room temperature
2 tablespoons fresh lemon juice
1 scant cup salad oil
2 teaspoons drained capers, dried with paper towels
4 pinches cayenne pepper
½ teaspoon salt
2 tablespoons finely chopped fresh parsley (stems removed)
2 teaspoons finely chopped green onion, green part only
1 tablespoon finely chopped sweet pickle, squeezed in paper towel to extract the liquid

SCALLOPS
Oil for lubricating scallops and greasing fish basket
2 pounds sea scallops

1. *Make Tartar Sauce:* Put egg yolks and lemon juice in food processor or blender container. Blend for 2–3 seconds.
2. Turn motor on again and begin adding oil, drop by drop. After ½ cup has been added, begin adding oil in a very thin, steady stream, as slowly as possible, but still maintaining a flow of oil.
3. When oil has been added, mixture should be thick. Transfer to medium-size bowl.
4. Stir in capers, cayenne pepper, salt, parsley, green onion, and sweet pickle. Mix well.
5. *Grill scallops:* Oil scallops on both sides and arrange in a single layer in the bottom of a well-oiled fish basket. Fasten top. Grill over ashen coals about 2 minutes on each side or until scallops are just done.
6. Remove from grill and transfer scallops to large, round, heated serving platter, leaving space in center for bowl of tartar sauce. Serve immediately.

Yield: 4 servings

SEA SCALLOPS WITH ORIENTAL VEGETABLES

1½–1¾ pounds sea scallops
Peanut oil for lubricating scallops and greasing grill
2   tablespoons peanut oil
½   teaspoon each: garlic powder and ground gingerroot
3   green onions, chopped
4   Chinese mushrooms (available at Oriental food markets),
     reconstituted for 10 minutes in hot water and drained
¼   cup canned sliced water chestnuts, drained
2   tablespoons soy sauce
1   teaspoon sesame oil
Salt and pepper to taste

1. Brush sea scallops with peanut oil. Arrange scallops in a prepared double-hinged fish basket. Grill scallops for 3–4 minutes. Brush scallops with oil and turn over. Continue grilling until scallops become opaque. Place on a heated platter.

2. Heat the 2 tablespoons peanut oil in a wok or a heavy skillet. Sprinkle oil with garlic and ginger. Stir-fry onions in the skillet until soft, about 1 minute. Mix in mushrooms and water chestnuts and stir-fry for 1 minute. Mix in seasonings. Pour vegetables over sea scallops. Serve with Rice Pilaf.

Yield: 4 servings

RICE PILAF

½ cup of egg noodles, cooked
⅓ cup butter
2 cups uncooked long-grain rice
4 cups chicken stock
Salt and pepper to taste

Sauté noodles in butter in a large skillet until noodles just turn brown, stirring often. Add the uncooked rice and stir. Add chicken stock and simmer, stirring occasionally, until the stock is absorbed and the rice is tender (approximately 18 minutes). Cover and let sit for three minutes before serving. Season to taste with salt and pepper and serve with Sea Scallops with Oriental Vegetables.

SHARK

Shark is a firm fish; it should be soaked in milk for 1 hour before cooking. Swordfish can be substituted in all shark recipes.

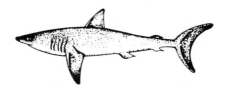

SHARK KABOBS WITH ORANGE AND THYME

Feel free to be creative. Add and change fruits and vegetables as desired.

ORANGE SAUCE
8 tablespoons (1 stick) butter
2 large shallots, minced
1 tablespoon grated orange zest
½ cup fresh orange juice

KABOBS
2 pounds shark steaks, cut into 1½-inch pieces
Milk
2 medium zucchini, cut into 1½-inch pieces
12 pearl onions, blanched in boiling water for 2 minutes
2 oranges, quartered
Peanut oil
2 tablespoons crumbled dried thyme

1. *Make sauce:* Melt butter in a saucepan over medium heat. Sauté shallots in it until tender, stirring occasionally. Whisk in orange zest and juice. Bring mixture to a boil, stir, and remove from heat. Reheat sauce when ready to serve.

2. *Grill shark kabobs:* Soak shark cubes in milk for 1 hour before grilling. Drain fish and pat dry with paper toweling. Thread 4 10″ skewers with fish, zucchini, onions, and orange quarters. Brush with peanut oil and sprinkle with 1 tablespoon of the thyme. Sprinkle remaining thyme over hot coals. Grill kabobs, rotating every 3 minutes until shark cubes begin to flake when tested with a fork. Serve on individual plates and allow guests to remove food from individual skewers. Pass warm Orange Sauce at table. Serve with buttered noodles.

Yield: 4 servings

Do you have some leftover fish, fruit, and/or vegetables? Be creative—kabob! Any firm-fleshed fish, such as shark, swordfish, tuna, scallops, or scrod (sole, flounder, or whitefish are too delicate) will do. Mix and match firm, flavorful fruits and vegetables as you please. The fruits and vegetables will cook at the same rate as the fish. Just brush with oil, grill, and enjoy.

SHRIMP

Shrimp, medium to firm texture, are delicious but tricky on the grill. Shrimp are cooked and ready to eat when they turn opaque; be careful not to overcook, for they will become tough.

CAJUN SHRIMP

1½ pounds large shrimp
1 tablespoon paprika
¼ teaspoon each: salt and freshly ground pepper
1 clove garlic, minced
8 tablespoons (1 stick) butter, melted
Oil for greasing grill
Lettuce leaves for garnish
Parsley sprigs for garnish

1. *Butterfly shrimp:* Leaving shell intact, slit underside of shrimp lengthwise, but don't cut all the way through. Remove legs.
2. *Marinate shrimp:* Combine paprika, salt, pepper, and garlic, and stir into melted butter. Pour mixture into a shallow dish. Add shrimp and stir to coat evenly. Marinate shrimp for 1 hour, turning once.
3. *Grill shrimp:* Shake off and reserve any extra marinade and arrange shrimp on prepared grill or in a double-hinged grill basket. Grill shrimp for 3–4 minutes, brush with reserved marinade, and continue cooking 1–2 minutes or until done. Arrange shrimp decoratively on a plate over lettuce leaves, garnish with parsley, and serve hot.

Yield: 4 servings

EAST INDIAN SHRIMP IN A TANDOORI MARINADE

4 pounds medium shrimp, shelled and deveined
16 ounces (2 8-ounce cartons) plain yogurt
6 tablespoons fresh lemon juice
1¼ teaspoons each: cayenne pepper, turmeric, and curry powder
4 teaspoons paprika
½ teaspoon salt
2 teaspoons finely minced or pressed garlic
2 teaspoons peeled and finely minced fresh gingerroot
Oil for greasing grill
Lemon wedges and chopped onions for garnish

1. Thread shrimp on 8 10" skewers and lay skewers on a jelly roll sheet or any pan that will hold them in one layer.

2. *Marinate shrimp:* In a small bowl, mix yogurt, lemon juice, cayenne pepper, turmeric, curry powder, paprika, salt, garlic, and ginger. Spoon yogurt mixture over skewered shrimp, covering completely. Slip into a plastic bag and refrigerate at least 6 hours.

3. *Grill shrimp:* Grill skewered shrimp over ashen coals for 3–4 minutes. Turn and continue cooking, about 3 minutes, until done. Serve immediately with lemon wedges and chopped onion.

Yield: 4 servings

INDONESIAN SHRIMP SATE WITH PEANUT SAUCE

This dish is very exciting. Serve it as an appetizer or entree.

PEANUT SAUCE

1   tablespoon oil
2   tablespoons finely chopped onion
2   large garlic cloves, minced
1   teaspoon peeled and chopped fresh gingerroot
½   teaspoon cayenne pepper
¾   teaspoon salt
⅛   teaspoon ground cumin
2   tablespoons soy sauce (use Japanese light soy, if possible)
3   tablespoons dark corn syrup
3   tablespoons fresh lemon juice
½   cup peanut butter
6   ounces canned coconut milk

MARINADE

2   tablespoons oil
6   cloves garlic, minced
2   tablespoons finely chopped onion
2   teaspoons turmeric
¼   teaspoon cayenne pepper
1   teaspoon salt
4   tablespoons peanut butter
8   tablespoons fresh lemon juice

SHRIMP

4   dozen medium shrimp, shelled and deveined
Oil for greasing grill
Lemon wedges for garnish

1. *Make sauce:* Heat 1 tablespoon oil in skillet. Add 2 tablespoons onion, 2 minced garlic cloves, and ginger and sauté for 3 minutes over low heat. Add ½ teaspoon cayenne, ¾ teaspoon salt, and the cumin. Sauté for 1 minute and transfer to bowl or food processor container.

2. Stir in soy sauce, corn syrup, 3 tablespoons lemon juice, ½ cup peanut butter, and the coconut milk. Mix very well. At serving time, if sauce is too thick, add additional coconut milk or lemon juice to thin to desired dipping consistency (serve at room temperature). Sauce will keep serveral days in the refrigerator if well covered.

3. *Marinate shrimp:* Thread shrimp onto 8 10″ skewers and lay in bottom of a large pan with raised sides.

4. Heat oil in a medium skillet. Add garlic, onion, turmeric, cayenne, and salt. Sauté over low heat for about 4 minutes.

5. Transfer to bowl or food processor container and mix with peanut butter and lemon juice. Spoon over skewered shrimp and marinate for 30–60 minutes.

6. *Grill shrimp:* Place shrimp on prepared grill and cook about 1 minute or until done on each side or until slightly charred.

7. Serve shrimp with ample lemon wedges. Pass Peanut Sauce.

Yield: 4 servings, with about 1¾ cups sauce

SHRIMP TOSTADAS WITH GUACAMOLE

GUACAMOLE

2   large ripe avocados
2   teaspoons fresh lime juice
½   teaspoon salt
2   green onions, cut into rough 1-inch lengths, both green and white parts
1   small tomato, peeled and quartered
1   clove garlic, halved
1   small fresh hot chili pepper, halved lengthwise and seeded

SHRIMP AND TOSTADAS

Oil for frying tortillas
8   fresh corn tortillas
32   medium shrimp
Oil for greasing grill
1   16-ounce can refried beans
2   tablespoons oil
Red Salsa (see index for recipe)
Small bowls of each of the following: chopped lettuce, chopped onion, chopped queso fresco (Mexican cheese), and chopped fresh cilantro or parsley

1. *Make guacamole:* Cut avocados in half and remove pits. Scoop avocado out of shell and place in container of food processor. Add lime juice; process until pureed.

2. Add salt, onion, tomato, garlic, and small hot pepper to avocado mixture; process again until finely pureed. Transfer to small bowl. Add avocado pits to bowl (they will help retard discoloration). Remove pits before bringing bowl to table.

3. *Fry tortillas:* Heat 1 inch of oil in a shallow 8" or 9" skillet. Slide tortillas one by one into oil and fry on each side until just golden. Remove immediately; drain on paper towels.

4. *Grill shrimp and prepare beans:* Meanwhile, thread shrimp onto 8 10" skewers and grill over ashen coals. While shrimp cook, transfer refried beans from can to saucepan, add 2 tablespoons oil, stir well, and heat over low heat.

5. When shrimp are cooked, remove from skewers, transfer to small dish, and bring to table.

6. Guests should make their own tostadas: Spread refried beans on top of a fried tostada. Arrange shrimp over this. Spoon red salsa and guacamole over top of shrimp. Then add a little shredded lettuce, chopped onion, and grated fresh Mexican cheese over the top. Top with some chopped fresh cilantro or parlsey.

Yield: 4 servings

SOLE

This is a delicate fish which will grill easily and quickly.
Substitutes include flounder and orange roughy.

DOVER SOLE WITH NORMANDY SAUCE

NORMANDY SAUCE
5   tablespoons butter
1   small onion, sliced thin
2   large apples, cored and sliced thin
½   cup apple cider or juice
Salt and white pepper to taste
1   cup heavy cream

FISH
4   7-ounce Dover sole fillets
Melted butter
Oil for greasing fish basket
1   apple, cored and sliced, for garnish

   1. *Make sauce:* Melt 5 tablespoons butter in a saucepan. Sauté
onion in it until tender. Add the 2 sliced apples and cook for 1
minute, stirring occasionally. Blend in cider and salt and pepper
to taste. Cook until mixture has been reduced by half. Stir in
cream and simmer until sauce is warm. Remove saucepan from
heat and reheat when ready to serve.
   2. *Grill Dover sole:* Brush Dover sole fillets with melted butter
and arrange in a prepared double-hinged fish basket. Secure
basket and cook fillets about 3–4 minutes. Continue grilling about
2–3 minutes, depending on thickness of fish, until sole begins to
flake when tested with a fork. Arrange fillets on individual plates
and drizzle sauce around fish. Garnish with a sliced apple.

Yield: 4 servings

SOLE AND SALMON BUNDLES

This dish can be called chinois—*a combination of French style (Sole Stuffed with Salmon) and oriental presentation.*

½ pound salmon fillet, skinned and cut into ½-by-2½-inch pieces
4 green onions, 2 halved horizontally and remaining 2 cut lengthwise into thirds
4 7-ounce sole fillets
Crumbled dried tarragon
Melted butter
Oil for greasing grill
1 lime, cut into wedges, for garnish

With a pair of tweezers reserved for kitchen use, remove all visible bones from salmon. Place one piece of salmon and a green onion half on the end of each sole fillet. Sprinkle with tarragon to taste. Roll the sole, jelly-roll style, forming a bundle. Tie each bundle securely with a long green onion strip. Brush sole with melted butter and place on prepared grill. Cook for 4–6 minutes. Brush and turn and continue grilling 2–3 minutes, depending on thickness of fish, until fish begins to flake when tested with a fork. Place seafood bundles on individual plates and serve with lime wedges and cooked fresh asparagus.

Yield: 4 servings

STRIPED BASS

A medium-firm fish with a mild flavor and low fat content. Black sea bass, orange roughy, and ocean perch taste great in striped bass recipes.

STRIPED BASS MARINATED IN THE KOREAN MANNER

MARINADE

¼ cup soy sauce
2 tablespoons sugar
1 tablespoon finely minced garlic
1 tablespoon finely minced green onions, green part only
2 tablespoons oil
2 tablespoons sesame seeds

FISH

4 striped bass fillets (about 2 pounds), each cut into 2 pieces, skin on
Oil for greasing grill

1. *Prepare marinade:* Combine soy sauce, sugar, garlic, green onion, and oil. Put sesame seeds in a medium-size frying pan and set over medium heat. Stir for a moment or two or until they begin to brown. Add to soy sauce mixture.

2. *Marinate striped bass:* Lay fillets skin side down in a single layer in a pan with raised sides. Pour soy mixture over fillets. Let sit for a moment, then turn fillets so they are flesh side down. Refrigerate, covered, for 30 minutes.

3. *Grill striped bass:* At serving time, remove from marinade and place bass on prepared grill over ashen coals, skin side touching grill, for 3–4 minutes on one side only. (Do not turn fillets or they will fall apart.) Baste fillet with marinade every minute or so until done. Use a greased spatula to transfer fish to serving platter.

Yield: 4 servings

WHOLE STRIPED BASS IN THE STYLE OF SOLONIKA

This fish is served on a bed of chopped parsley and onions in a classic Greek style.

SOLONIKA DRESSING

¼ cup olive oil
1 cup firmly packed chopped fresh parsley sprigs
1 medium onion, sliced thin

FISH

¼ cup olive oil
¼ cup fresh lemon juice
¼ teaspoon each: salt and freshly ground black pepper
1 teaspoon crumbled dried oregano
4 small striped bass or snapper fillets, head and tail intact
Grapevine pieces (optional), available in Greek food stores or
    backyard if you have grapevines
Oil for greasing grill
Greek olives for garnish

    1. *Make dressing:* Toss dressing ingredients together in small bowl. Cover and refrigerate until ready to serve.
    2. *Grill striped bass:* Combine ¼ cup olive oil, the lemon juice, and the seasonings. Rub the outside and cavity of the fish with seasoning mixture. Place 2 foot-long pieces of grapevine over the hot coals. Arrange fish in an oiled double-hinged fish basket. Place basket over grill and cook for 5–7 minutes. Baste with remaining seasoning mixture and continue cooking 2–3 minutes, depending on thickness of fish, until fish begins to flake when tested with a fork. Place dressing on bottom of serving platter and arrange fish over it. Sprinkle fish with olives.

Yield: 4 servings

SWORDFISH

A favorite for grilling. It is a firm, mildly distinct fish. Substitute
shark or tuna; recipes will work but taste will be different.

SWORDFISH KABOBS
WITH MIDDLE EASTERN DIPPING SAUCES

TARAMOSALATA
1 small onion, quartered
6 slices white bread, crusts removed
1 cup water
½ cup (4 ounces) tarama (salted carp roe, available at specialty
   food stores)
3 tablespoons fresh lemon juice
1 cup olive oil

HUMMUS
2 cloves garlic
1 small onion, quartered
1 19-ounce can chick-peas, drained
½ cup tahini (sesame seed paste, available at specialty food
   stores)
2 tablespoons fresh lemon juice
3 tablespoons olive oil
Salt to taste

FISH
1½ pounds swordfish cut into 1-inch chunks
12 cherry tomatoes
Oil for greasing grill

1. *Make Taramosalata:* Using a blender or a food processor fitted with a steel blade, puree quartered onion. Soak bread in water for 4–5 minutes. Squeeze bread dry and discard water. Add bread to machine and puree. Place tarama and 3 tablespoons lemon juice in work bowl with onion and bread and puree. With the machine running, pour in 1 cup olive oil through the feed tube in a slow steady stream until it is incorporated. Taste Taramosalata and adjust seasonings. Store in a covered container and chill until ready to serve.

2. *Make Hummus:* Using a food processor fitted with a steel blade, mince garlic and quartered onion. Add remaining Hummus ingredients and puree. Taste and adjust seasonings. Store Hummus in a covered container and chill until ready to serve.

3. *Grill swordfish:* Thread 4 10″ skewers alternately with swordfish and cherry tomatoes. Cook, turning every 3 minutes until done. Serve immediately and pass dipping sauces (room temperature) at the table. Serve with warm pita bread.

Yield: 4 servings

SWORDFISH IN A TABASCO-BUTTERMILK MARINADE

4   cups buttermilk
1   tablespoon Tabasco sauce
4   swordfish steaks, cut 1 inch thick
Oil for greasing grill
Salt

1. *Marinate swordfish:* Mix buttermilk and Tabasco sauce together. Cut skin off swordfish steaks and pierce each in several places on both sides with the tines of a fork.

2. Lay a large plastic bag inside a bowl and open the top. Pour marinade into plastic bag, then add steaks. Close bag with twister seal and place in refrigerator for 3 hours.

3. *Grill swordfish:* At serving time, remove from marinade and place swordfish on oiled grill over ashen coals. Cook about 5 minutes on each side or until swordfish begins to flake when tested with a fork. Salt lightly and serve immediately.

Yield: 4 servings

Marinating is always easier in a plastic bag. Open a large bag and lay it on a bowl so that the mouth is open and the edges of the bag hang over the bowl on all sides. Add the fish and the marinade. Secure the bag with a twister seal and refrigerate. Don't forget to turn the bag often. The fish will be exposed to the marinade as much as possible, your refrigerator won't smell of either fish or marinade, and you won't have to wash the bowl.

SWORDFISH STEAKS WITH BARBECUE SAUCE

Swordfish will convince even the die-hard meat-eater that fish can be an immensely satisfying dish. There is not a bone or sinew in sight, just thick, meaty eating.

BARBECUE SAUCE
3   tablespoons oil
1   cup very finely chopped onion
4   garlic cloves, minced fine or pressed
1–2 small fresh hot peppers, seeded and chopped fine
1   cup canned tomato sauce
⅓   cup each: Worcestershire sauce and brown sugar
⅔   cup red wine vinegar
¼   teaspoon salt
2   pinches dried rosemary
1   pinch dried thyme
⅛   teaspoon Liquid Smoke
Tabasco sauce to taste (optional)

FISH
Oil for lubricating fish and greasing grill
4   swordfish steaks, each 1-inch thick

1. *Make sauce:* Heat 3 tablespoons oil in large frying pan. Sauté onion, garlic, and peppers in it for about 10 minutes over moderate heat, stirring often. Add tomato sauce, Worcestershire sauce, brown sugar, red wine vinegar, salt, rosemary, and thyme. Heat to boil, reduce heat, and simmer for about 5 minutes. Stir in Liquid Smoke. Taste and adjust seasoning, adding Tabasco if a hotter flavor is desired.

2. *Grill swordfish steaks:* Meanwhile, oil swordfish steaks on both sides. Then grease grill. Set fish on grill over ashen coals. Cook for 5–6 minutes on each side or until fish just flakes when tested with a fork. Serve immediately with Barbecue Sauce spooned over the top. Pass remaining Barbecue Sauce.

Yield: 4 servings

SWORDFISH WITH CANTONESE SAUCE

CANTONESE SAUCE
¼ cup dry white wine
½ teaspoon black soy sauce
1 teaspoon sesame oil

FISH
1 teaspoon minced fresh gingerroot
Grated zest of 1 orange
4 green onions, minced
4 7-ounce swordfish steaks
Peanut oil for lubricating fish and greasing grill
2 medium cucumbers, sliced horizontally, for garnish
¼ cup minced fresh cilantro (coriander), for garnish
4 green onions, cut into 1½-inch slivers, for garnish
Grated zest of 1 orange, for garnish

    1. *Make sauce:* Mix together wine, soy sauce, and sesame oil in a small bowl. Cover sauce and set aside.
    2. *Grill swordfish:* Mix together ginger, zest of 1 orange, and green onions. Brush fish with oil and sprinkle with ginger mixture. Arrange swordfish steaks on prepared grill. Cook for 5–6 minutes. Turn fish over with a spatula and continue cooking 2–3 minutes, depending on thickness of fish, until fish begins to flake when tested with a fork. Place swordfish on platter and drizzle sauce over fish. Decoratively arrange cucumbers, cilantro, onions, and zest of 1 orange over fish. Serve hot or cold.

Yield: 4 servings

SWORDFISH WITH HOMEMADE LEMON MAYONNAISE

LEMON MAYONNAISE
1   egg plus 1 egg yolk, room temperature
3   tablespoons fresh lemon juice
1   cup salad oil
½   teaspoon salt
Big pinch cayenne pepper
Finely grated zest of 1 lemon

FISH
Oil for lubricating fish and greasing grill
4   swordfish steaks, each 1 inch thick

1. *Make mayonnaise:* Put egg and yolk in container of food processor or blender along with lemon juice, 2 tablespoons of the oil, the salt, cayenne pepper, and lemon zest. Blend for a few seconds. With machine on, add remaining oil as slowly as possible in a very thin (less than ⅛ inch thick) but steady stream. When all oil has been added, mayonnaise will be thickened. Transfer to serving bowl.

2. *Grill swordfish steaks:* Oil swordfish steaks liberally on both sides. Place swordfish steaks on oiled grill for about 5 minutes on each side or until fish flesh has turned white. Watch carefully and do not overcook. Serve steaks with Lemon Mayonnaise.

Yield: 4 servings

TROUT

Brook trout, lake trout, and rainbow trout are medium-firm fish, medium flavored and high in fat content. Each can be substituted for the other.

INDIVIDUAL TROUTS WITH ARMENIAN STUFFING

FISH
4   whole fresh trout, about 8–10 ounces each, boned, scaled, fins removed, heads and tails intact
White wine to cover trout
Oil for lubricating fish and greasing fish basket

STUFFING
4   tablespoons (½ stick) butter
4   medium onions, chopped fine
⅔   cup each: pine nuts and currants
Scant ½ teaspoon each: cinnamon, allspice, and salt
1   tablespoon chopped fresh parsley
2½ teaspoons fresh lemon juice
Large pinch cayenne pepper

1. *Marinate trout:* Lay trout in a shallow nonmetallic dish with raised sides. Cover with dry white wine (jug wine is perfectly acceptable). Let sit for 30 minutes.

2. *Make stuffing:* Melt butter in a medium frying pan over low heat. Sauté onions for 10 minutes, stirring often. Then stir in pine nuts, currants, cinnamon, allspice, salt, parsley, lemon juice, and cayenne pepper. Mix well and cook for another minute. Remove from heat and allow to cool, about 10 minutes.

3. *Stuff fish:* Remove fish from white wine, shake to remove excess, and oil them well on both sides. Divide stuffing evenly among fish, patting it into center of fish.

4. *Grill trout:* Lay all four fish in well-oiled fish basket (or lay them on well-oiled grill) and fasten top of basket. Cook fish for 6–7 minutes on each side or until fish has turned white and is beginning to flake. Serve immediately.

Yield: 4 servings

Keep a pair of tweezers in the kitchen. This way, you can remove bones anytime you find them. You might try running your hand along an uncooked fillet to feel for bones before putting it on the grill.

WHOLE TROUT WITH ROSEMARY AND SAGE

Double flavor, inside and out, with lime slices and rosemary sprinkled over the hot coals in the French style.

1   tablespoon dried leaf rosemary
1   tablespoon rubbed sage
½   teaspoon freshly ground pepper
¼   cup olive oil
1   3½-pound lake trout or four individual rainbow trout, 8–10
     ounces each, cleaned, head and tail intact
1   large lime, sliced
1   tablespoon dried leaf rosemary
Oil for greasing grill

    1. Combine 1 tablespoon rosemary, the sage, and the pepper with olive oil. Rub the trout, including the cavity, with the herb mixture. Place lime slices in the cavity.

    2. Sprinkle remaining rosemary over coals. Place trout on prepared grill or on a double layer of greased aluminum foil with a few holes poked in it. Grill for 5–6 minutes on each side or until the fish begins to flake when tested with a fork. Baste fish during cooking. With a greased spatula, carefully transfer trout to platter. Serve with a pasta salad.

Yield: 4 servings

TUNA

A firm fish high in fat content. Substitute swordfish when tuna is not available.

TUNA WITH GREEN SALSA

GREEN SALSA

1 10-ounce can tomatillos (green husk tomatotes, available in Mexican food stores), including juice
1 medium onion, quartered
1 clove garlic
2 mild chili peppers, seeded and chopped
¼ cup chopped fresh cilantro (coriander)
1 small hot pepper, or to taste, seeded and chopped (optional)

FISH

4 7-ounce tuna fillets
Peanut oil for lubricating fish and greasing fish basket
1 cup chopped fresh cilantro (coriander)

1. *Make salsa:* Puree all salsa ingredients in a food processor fitted with a steel blade or in a blender. Cover and refrigerate until ready to serve.

2. *Grill tuna:* Brush tuna with peanut oil. Arrange half of the cilantro in prepared grill basket and place fish on top. Cover with remaining cilantro. Secure basket. Grill for 5 minutes. Turn basket and continue cooking until fish begins to flake when tested with a fork. Slightly undercook tuna. Transfer to individual plates. Pass Green Salsa at the table and serve with warm flour tortillas that have been wrapped in aluminum foil and stacked in a 350°F oven for 15 minutes. Eat tortillas as you would bread, spread with butter.

Yield: 4 servings

GRILLED TUNA SALAD NICOISE

Once you've had grilled tuna, you'll never want to open a can again. Try this delectable salad with simple Garlic Bread.

VINAIGRETTE
¾ cup good-quality imported olive oil
⅓ cup red wine vinegar
2 teaspoons Dijon mustard
2 teaspoons snipped fresh chives
¾ teaspoon each: dried rosemary and salt

SALAD
1 pound small round boiling potatoes
1 head Boston lettuce, washed, dried, leaves separated
8 ounces green beans, cooked and chilled
3 medium eggs, hard-boiled and quartered lengthwise
4 firm fresh plum tomatoes, quartered lengthwise
Oil for lubricating tuna and greasing grill
8 ounces fresh tuna
8 flat anchovy fillets, drained
½ cup jumbo pitted black olives, drained
2 tablespoons finely chopped fresh parsley

1. *Make vinaigrette:* Combine ¾ cup oil, the vinegar, mustard, chives, tarragon, and salt in a medium bowl.
2. *Marinate potatoes:* Put potatoes in a saucepan and add water to cover. Heat to boiling, lower heat to simmer, and cook until soft enough to be pierced with a fork. When potatoes are cooked, drain and peel. Carefully add hot potatoes to bowl in which vinaigrette has been sitting and spoon some vinaigrette over potatoes. Let sit in vinaigrette until ready to use.
3. *Prepare vegetables:* Use Boston lettuce leaves to line a glass bowl. Then arrange green beans, eggs, and tomatoes in individual piles over lettuce. Carefully remove potatoes from vinaigrette and arrange them in a pile on lettuce.
4. *Grill tuna:* Oil tuna on both sides and cook on oiled grill over ashen coals for about 4 minutes on each side or until tuna is almost cooked. Do not cook tuna all the way through; it should be served rare, like roast beef. Separate cooled tuna into small

chunks with a fork and arrange in a pile on lettuce.

5. *Dress and garnish:* Lay anchovy fillets and black olives over top of entire salad. Then pour remaining vinaigrette over salad. Sprinkle with parsley and serve immediately.

Yield: 4 servings

GARLIC BREAD

6 tablespoons butter
3 cloves garlic
1 loaf French bread, sliced horizontally

1. Melt butter with garlic over medium heat.
2. Brush butter over cut bread, then wrap in aluminum foil. Heat on grill for five minutes, turn once, and continue heating three minutes more. Remove from grill, slice, and serve with Grilled Tuna Salad Niçoise.

GRILLED TUNA SALAD
WITH CAPERS AND HOMEMADE MAYONNAISE

MAYONNAISE
1   egg plus 1 egg yolk, room temperature
3   tablespoons cider vinegar
½   teaspoon salt
Large pinch cayenne pepper
1   cup oil

SALAD
Oil for lubricating fish and greasing grill
8   ounces fresh tuna
1   tablespoon drained capers
2   tablespoons finely chopped fresh parsley

1. *Make mayonnaise:* Put egg and egg yolk in food processor or blender container along with vinegar, salt, cayenne pepper, and 2 tablespoons of the oil. Process for about 6 seconds as necessary.

2. Turn on motor and begin adding remaining oil. Add oil in a very thin (no more than ⅛ inch thick), steady stream. Keep motor running until all oil is added, then turn off motor. Let sit at room temperature for 5 minutes.

3. *Grill tuna:* Oil tuna on both sides and place on prepared grill for about 4 minutes on each side or until tuna is almost cooked. Tuna should always be cooked slightly rare like roast beef, so watch carefully.

4. *Assemble salad:* Let tuna cool to room temperature or until just warm. Separate tuna into small, irregular chunks with a fork and place in a glass bowl. Add ⅔ cup of the mayonnaise and mix well. Then mix in capers. Top with parsley. Serve at room temperature.

Yield: 4 servings; 1⅔ cups mayonnaise (Leftover homemade mayonnaise, if covered, will keep at least 2 days in refrigerator.)

TUNA WITH ORIENTAL BARBECUE SAUCE

BARBECUE SAUCE
¼ cup hoisin sauce (available at Oriental food markets)
1 teaspoon sugar
1 teaspoon sesame oil
2 cloves garlic, minced

FISH
4 7-ounce tuna steaks
Oil for greasing grill or fish basket
1 cup snow peas (fresh, if possible), trimmed, for garnish

1. *Make sauce:* Combine hoisin sauce, sugar, and sesame oil in a small saucepan. Simmer, stirring often over low heat, for 2 minutes. Remove saucepan from heat and cool sauce.

2. *Grill tuna:* Brush tuna steaks with barbecue sauce and place in a prepared double-hinged wire grill basket or cook directly on prepared grill. Cook tuna for 5–6 minutes. Brush steaks with sauce and turn. Continue grilling 2–3 minutes or until fish begins to flake when tested with a fork. Tuna should be cooked like roast beef, only until slightly pink in the center. Place tuna on individual dishes and sprinkle with snow peas for garnish.

Yield: 4 servings

WHITEFISH

A medium-flavored fish that can be substituted with salmon or haddock. Both fillets and whole fish work well on the grill.

ORANGE WHITEFISH

MARINADE
¼ cup peanut oil
2   tablespoons minced fresh parlsey
1   tablespoon fresh lemon juice
Juice of 1 orange

FISH
4   7-ounce whitefish fillets
2   tablespoons grated orange zest
Oil for greasing grill
2   large oranges, sliced

1. *Marinate whitefish:* Combine all marinade ingredients and place in a shallow glass dish. Marinate whitefish fillets for 1 hour, turning once. Drain whitefish and reserve marinade.

2. *Grill whitefish:* Sprinkle fillets with orange zest and place on prepared grill. Cook for 4–5 minutes. Turn fish and continue grilling for 2–3 minutes, depending on thickness of fish, or until it begins to flake easily when tested with a fork. Place orange slices on grill and cook on both sides for 2–4 minutes. Place fish on individual serving plates and top with orange slices. Serve with a large green salad.

Yield: 4 servings

WHITEFISH DE JONGHE

STUFFING

4 tablespoons butter, softened
½ teaspoon each: finely chopped garlic, finely chopped onion, and finely chopped fresh hot pepper
¼ teaspoon salt
1 pinch dried thyme
1 tablespoon finely chopped fresh parlsey (stems removed)
2–3 tablespoons sherry
1½ cups bread crumbs
4 tablespoons finely chopped blanched almonds

FISH

Oil for lubricating fish and greasing fish basket
1 3-pound whole whitefish, scaled and boned
4 slices lemon

    1. *Stuff whitefish:* Mix butter with garlic, onion, hot pepper, salt, thyme, and parsley. Add sherry, bread crumbs, and chopped almonds, stirring well. Stuff whitefish with the mixture.

    2. *Grill whitefish:* Oil whitefish on both sides, then oil inside of fish basket. Arrange 2 slices of lemon on grill basket bottom. Arrange fish over lemon slices. Top fish with remaining 2 lemon slices and fasten top of grill basket. Place on grill over ashen coals and grill 6–7 minutes on each side, or until it begins to flake easily when tested with a fork. Serve immediately.

Yield: 4 servings

BUTTERFLIED WHITEFISH IN A CRUMB CRUST

MARINADE
½ cup oil
1   tablespoon fresh lemon juice
¼ teaspoon Tabasco sauce

FISH
1   2½- to 3-pound whole whitefish, boned and butterflied

COATING
½ cup each: chopped cashews and bread crumbs
⅓ cup grated Parmesan cheese
2   cloves garlic, minced fine
¼ teaspoon salt
Oil for greasing fish basket
8   slices lemon

1. *Marinate whitefish:* Mix ½ cup oil, the lemon juice, and Tabasco sauce in small bowl. Open fish butterfly fashion and lay in a flat dish with raised sides. Pour marinade over fish. Let sit, covered, for 30 minutes in refrigerator.

2. *Stuff whitefish:* Meanwhile, mix cashews, bread crumbs, Parmesan cheese, garlic, and salt in a small bowl.

3. When fish has marinated for 30 minutes, remove from marinade and lay, butterfly fashion, on a flat plate. Pat half of cashew mixture over top of fish. Turn fish, brush with marinade if it needs lubrication, and pat remaining half of cashew mixture over other side of fish.

4. *Grill whitefish:* Oil a fish basket and lay 4 lemon slices on bottom. Arrange fish, butterfly fashion, on lemon slices. Top with remaining 4 lemon slices. Attach top of fish basket. Put on grill over ashen coals. Cook for 3–4 minutes on each side or until crumbs are lightly browned and fish flakes easily when tested with a fork. Serve immediately with Homemade Baked Beans.

Yield: 4 servings

HOMEMADE BAKED BEANS

1 pound small dried white or red beans
¼ pound lean salt pork, cut into small cubes
½ pound smoked ham, cut into ½-inch cubes
1¼ cups light or dark brown sugar
3 cups water
1 onion, quartered
1 large bay leaf
2 garlic cloves, peeled
1½ teaspoons each: salt, dry mustard, and dried crushed red
    pepper
1 teaspoon each: ground coriander and freshly ground black
    pepper
⅛ teaspoon each: ground nutmeg, ground cinnamon, celery salt,
    ground allspice, and dried leaf rosemary
Small handful fresh parsley, stems removed

1. Wash beans under running water and heat to boil in a saucepan with water to cover. Simmer 10 minutes. Drain and put beans in a 10-cup bean pot or any baking dish with a cover.

2. Stir salt pork and ham into beans. Then sprinkle brown sugar over top. Stir to combine.

3. Pour 3 cups water into food processor or blender container. Then add onion, bay leaf, garlic, salt, dry mustard, red pepper, coriander, black pepper, nutmeg, cinnamon, celery salt, allspice, rosemary, and parsley. Blend until coarsely pureed. Pour over beans and mix to combine.

4. Cover bean pot and place in a 250°F oven for 8–10 hours. Be careful to check bean pot every hour, adding additional water and stirring well as needed. Beans should always be covered with liquid. Serve hot or cold with Butterflied Whitefish in a Crumb Crust. Beans can be reheated and will keep several days in the refrigerator.

Note: This recipe will yield al dente beans. If you like them softer, cook longer.

Yield: 8–10 servings

WHITEFISH FILLETS
WITH BEURRE BLANC SAUCE AND LIME

This is an all white entree: fish and sauce are both white. Serve it on colored plates with colorful accompaniments such as radicchio in the salad, broccoli or asparagus or a side dish of roasted red peppers.

BEURRE BLANC SAUCE
3   large shallots, minced
1   cup dry white wine
2   tablespoons fresh lime juice or white wine vinegar
16 tablespoons (2 sticks) butter, cut into ½ inch pieces

FISH
4   7-ounce whitefish fillets
Melted butter
Freshly ground white pepper
Oil for greasing grill
1   tablespoon grated lime zest
2   limes, quartered, for garnish

    1. *Make sauce:* Combine shallots, wine, and lime juice in a heavy nonaluminum saucepan and reduce mixture to 2–3 tablespoons. Remove saucepan from heat, add 2 pieces of the butter, and whisk until incorporated. Whisk in remaining butter, 2 pieces at a time, being careful not to allow the sauce to separate. If sauce separates, whisk quickly and try to emulsify. Keep sauce warm over simmering water or serve immediately.
    2. *Grill whitefish:* Brush whitefish fillets with melted butter and sprinkle with pepper. Arrange fish on prepared grill. If using the tail section, tuck tail under fish to help even the thickness. Cook for 4 minutes, brush with butter, and turn fish. Continue cooking 3 minutes or until done, depending on thickness of fish. Place on individual dishes and ladle sauce over fish. Sprinkle with lime zest. Serve whitefish fillets garnished with lime wedges.

Yield: 4 servings

WHITEFISH STUFFED WITH SHRIMP

Great for that special VIP dinner.

STUFFING
2 tablespoons butter
½ cup finely chopped onion
2 pinches cayenne pepper
¼ teaspoon each: salt and dried tarragon
12 medium-size cooked shrimp, peeled, deveined, and chopped coarse
1 cup bread crumbs

FISH
1 3-pound whole whitefish, scaled and boned
Oil for lubricating fish and greasing fish basket
4 slices lemon

1. *Stuff whitefish:* Melt butter in medium saucepan. Add onion and sauté for about 10 minutes over medium heat. Stir in cayenne pepper, salt, and tarragon and cook for another minute. Remove from heat and stir in shrimp and bread crumbs. Mix well, then use to fill whitefish cavity.
2. *Grill whitefish:* Oil fish well on both sides and oil inside of fish basket. Lay 2 lemon slices on bottom of grill basket. Lay fish in basket over lemon slices. Top fish with 2 more lemon slices. Fasten top of grill basket and put on grill over ashen coals. Cook 8–9 minutes on each side or until fish flakes easily when tested with a fork. Serve immediately.

Yield: 4 servings

WHITEFISH WITH GARLIC AND BLACK BEAN SAUCE

BLACK BEAN SAUCE
2   tablespoons peanut oil
1   tablespoon salted black beans, washed, drained, and mashed
    (available at Oriental food markets)
2   cloves garlic, minced
3   green onions, minced
1   teaspoon minced fresh gingerroot
3   tablespoons light soy sauce
3   tablespoons dry white wine
½   teaspoon sugar
6   tablespoons water
¼   teaspoon salt
1   teaspoon cornstarch, mixed with 1 teaspoon water

FISH
1   3½-pound whole whitefish or trout, scaled, head and tail intact
Peanut oil for lubricating fish and greasing grill

1. *Make sauce:* Heat 2 tablespoons oil in a small saucepan.
Stir in black beans, garlic, onions, and ginger. Combine remaining
sauce ingredients, except cornstarch mixture, in a small bowl. Stir
sauce into black beans. Blend in cornstarch mixture and continue
cooking until sauce begins to thicken, stirring often. Set sauce
aside.

2. *Grill whitefish:* Brush whitefish with peanut oil. Place fish
on prepared grill or on a double layer of aluminum foil, poked
with a few air holes. Grill for 6–7 minutes on each side. Arrange
fish on heated platter and drizzle warm sauce over fish. This
recipe is good hot or cold. Serve fish with rice.

Yield: 4–6 servings

INDEX